LIVE IT
STRONG

LIVE IT SERIES

LIVE IT
STRONG

TIM BAKER

 Fleming H. Revell

A Division of Baker Book House Co
Grand Rapids, Michigan 49516

© 2003 by Tim Baker

Published by Fleming H. Revell
a division of Baker Book House Company
P.O. Box 6287, Grand Rapids, MI 49516-6287
www.bakerbooks.com

Printed in the United States of America

Library of Congress Cataloging-in-Publication Data is on file at the Library of Congress, Washington, D.C.

ISBN 0-8007-5881-1

For Coley, Jess, and Jacob

CONTENTS

ACKNOWLEDGMENTS

Many thanks to

My kids, friends, and family and the students I've met along the way in youth ministry who have allowed me to use their stories or their influence in my life as material for this project.

The entire editorial staff at Baker Book House for their patience and hard work. Jennifer Leep, thanks for your willingness to take on these books. Wendy Wetzel, you are a great editor. Thanks for your amazing work on this manuscript.

Jacqui. Thanks for allowing me time to write this. You are an amazing wife!

INTRODUCTION

I'll never forget Chicken Legs.

Years ago when I thought it was cool to lift weights, pump iron, and do my best to out-bench-press the other weight room dudes, I ran into Chicken Legs. We were classmates, and through working out together we became fairly good friends.

Chicken Legs had looks that could stop a bus filled with single women. I know this because I'm the average-looking kind of guy who envies good-looking people and the influence they have over other people. This guy didn't just have a good-looking face, he also had a great body. His arms, chest, and abs were cut like no human I had ever seen. Girls would show up for basketball games just to watch him move up and down the court. They seemed to especially love it when he'd sweat a lot. When we worked out I would often be amazed at his physique and dream about crafting my body in much the same way.

But Chicken Legs had one physical flaw. He had, well, chicken legs. No joke. Walking around in only a pair of workout shorts, this guy looked like a Ken doll upper body rammed on top of two anorexic toothpicks. For some reason his upper body strength and perfect shape didn't match his lower body. It didn't seem to matter much to Chicken Legs, though. He just kept working out.

To his face and behind his back, many of us who worked out with him would tease Chicken Legs about this oddity. Not in a mean kind of way—more in a freaky circus sideshow fan kind of way. Seriously, if Chicken Legs ever needed money, he could easily have taken his mismatched body on the road. He could have made serious cash.

From watching this guy I learned that strength and weakness can often exist in the same person. Chicken Legs, with his weird pencil-like lower half, taught me that one person can be both strong and weak. I learned that no one is perfectly strong or completely weak. All of us are out of balance. We have areas in our lives where we are amazingly strong. We also have areas in our lives where we are uncontrollably weak.

That's why we need a Savior.

Look, you're an oddball. You're a Chicken Legs, and honestly, so am I. We have areas in our lives where we are incredibly weak. And we need a Savior to come along with us, show us our weak areas, and walk with us as we strengthen our weaknesses. God can't stand to see you stumbling around with your toothpick-sized spiritual legs. He's just as frustrated with your weakness as you are.

Live It Strong is designed to help you build up your spiritual pencil legs, work on your spiritual body, and beef up your soul. This book is about putting your body, attitude, heart, and power in God's hands. In his hands, you can become strong. In his hands, you will be confident and powerful.

How do you use this book?

This book is put together so you can use it in two ways. You can pick it up and read a couple of pages from anywhere in the book for your devotions. Or you can start at the beginning and read the devotionals in order, one a day. If you do that for a few days, you'll begin to notice the following pattern:

Day 1: This day introduces a topic and usually asks you to write down your own ideas about it after reflecting on Scripture.

Days 2–5: These days take different angles to help you understand more about the topic.

Day 6: This day gives you a situation you might encounter and asks you to try to apply what you've learned through the week to the topic.

Day 7: The last day of the week you get to do a simple activity that helps illustrate the theme for the week.

It doesn't really matter how you use this book. Do whatever works for you. But before you start, here's a little advice about having devotions.

1. **Find a good time.** You've got to read God's Word when you're most awake and alert. Some people are awake at 6:30 A.M., and they're firing on all their cylinders. Truth is, not everyone is like that. If you aren't alert in the morning, don't have devos then. Think about when you're most alert, and give God your time when he'll get you at your best.
2. **Learn your own way.** You're not a copy. Everyone doesn't learn the same way or in the same environment. Do your friends tell you they read the Bible before they go to bed? Have you ever wondered why you don't remember anything you read before you go to bed, but your friends do? Maybe your bed isn't the best place for you to read. Give some thought to the best place for you to read God's Word. Find a place where you'll be able to focus.
3. **Pray.** People talk a lot about how important it is to have prayer after devotions. Truth is, prayer at the beginning is important too. Before you open God's Word, remember to ask him to guide your mind to what he wants you to learn.
4. **Mark where you've been.** Always keep a pencil handy. Keep one in your Bible. As you read through God's Word, mark things you think are interesting. If you do that, you'll know where you've been, and over time you'll create some valuable notes in your Bible.

The most important thing about devotions is simply that you have them. It's a tough discipline to keep a schedule of reading God's Word! *Live It Strong* will help you stay consistent in your devotional life and will challenge you to live God's Word without fear.

God bless you in your journey through this book and in your walk with Christ.

WHY SHOULD I BE LIKE JESUS?

God's Word

Do you not know? Have you not heard? The LORD is the everlasting God, the Creator of the ends of the earth. He will not grow tired or weary, and his understanding no one can fathom. Isaiah 40:28

I have testimony weightier than that of John. For the very work that the Father has given me to finish, and which I am doing, testifies that the Father has sent me. And the Father who sent me has himself testified concerning me. You have never heard his voice nor seen his form, nor does his word dwell in you, for you do not believe the one he sent. John 5:36–38

This is the message we have heard from him and declare to you: God is light; in him there is no darkness at all. 1 John 1:5

Live It

You love it when he does this.

Your dad is your hero. You admire him so much that you study everything he does. Most nights when your dad comes home from work, he heads straight to his chair with the newspaper and a Coke.

But tonight is different. Your dad came home and immediately took his tie off and put on a playful, menacing grin. You and your dad hit the floor in a no limits, all-out wrestling match. After you've whaled all over him, the two of you lay on the floor staring at the ceiling. Then your dad springs to his feet and stands with his hands out.

"Remember when you were little?"

"Dad, no! This is stupid."

"Come on," your dad says. "It'll be fun. Like old times."

Staring at your dad with one of those "I can't believe I'm doing this" looks, you walk to him and turn your back to him. Placing your hands in his, you step onto his feet. Slowly the two of you walk in step around the house, with your feet carefully balanced on his.

"Just like old times, huh?" your dad asks.

"Just like old times."

You and your dad both laugh as you fumble around the house. You feel like you're three years old again, and you honestly don't care how silly you look.

Walking with Jesus is a lot like walking with your dad—putting your feet on his and letting him carry you. You want to be this close to him so imitating him becomes second nature. You want to be just like Jesus.

So what does it mean to be like Jesus? Do you have to follow special rules and regulations? Are you supposed to wear certain clothes? Have you ever thought about what it means to follow Jesus? If you have, write down some of your ideas on these lines.

1. _____
2. _____
3. _____

This week we're going to toss around the tough and seemingly impossible task of being like Jesus. It's easy to say, "Be like Jesus," but it feels nearly impossible to do. So for the next six days we'll tackle this difficult task and learn what it means to walk exactly like the Savior.

Live It Strong

- Why is living like Jesus important?
- What things in your life make it difficult to imitate Jesus' actions in your life?
- What can you do this week to better imitate Jesus?

17

God's Word

Be perfect, therefore, as your heavenly Father is perfect. Matthew 5:48

Be merciful, just as your Father is merciful. Luke 6:36

Be imitators of God, therefore, as dearly loved children and live a life of love, just as Christ loved us and gave himself up for us as a fragrant offering and sacrifice to God. Ephesians 5:1–2

Live It

Do you know your dad? Do you like him?

That's really not a silly question. The more students I meet, the more tell me that they don't really know their parents. Many people grow up knowing *about* their parents but not actually knowing them.

Honestly, I knew *about* my dad more than I really knew him. He was a big, untouchable kind of figure in my life. My dad could fix anything. My dad could create anything. Give him a pencil and paper, and my dad could draw you an award-winning work of art. Give him a wrench, and he could repair my car. Give my dad a hardhat and a blueprint, and he could manage a multi-million dollar restoration project for the government.

My dad could do anything.

As a kid I always wanted to be like my dad. When my dad was young, he raced bikes, so I wanted to race bikes. My dad was an artist when I was young, and I wanted to be an artist too. My dad had a knack with facts, figures, and deep thinking, and I wanted to do the same thinking.

I'll never forget the moment I realized that I wasn't like my father. I wasn't unskilled or lacking in abilities. I just lacked the abilities and skills of my father. Over time I realized that while I can't do things *exactly* like my dad, I can do things somewhat like him. I realized that I liked bike racing, but not the kind he liked. So I raced BMX bikes. I realized that I wasn't an artist. I couldn't paint or draw, so I chose to make an attempt at using words to create images and motivate people.

18

I realized that I didn't have the knack for facts and figures exactly like my dad. Instead, I learned to gather information and remember facts differently. I was constantly striving to be just like my dad. In the end I've realized that I'm an imitation of my father. He can do things that I can't. My goal is to do things like him.

When I think of my relationship with God, I realize that it isn't much like me striving to be like my dad. I can't be God, and because of my sinful state, I can't be exactly like him.

But I can *strive* to be like him. I can't save myself, but I can give myself to him to be saved. I can't save others, but I can tell others about him and lead them to my saving Father. I can't create like God, but God has given me abilities to create unique things. Nope. I can't be God. But I can try my hardest to be an exact copy. I can do everything I can to know what he's like and then imitate him.

What about you?

God has set a standard for you. Not one filled with getting straight A's or making sure you get the best job possible. No, our first responsibility is to be exactly like our heavenly Father. The more we are like him, the more people will see him. The more people see him, the more come to know him.

Do you see how important it is to be like God?

Today, look at Jesus. He's actually waiting for you to look at him. Notice his character. See his attitude toward the world. Then imitate, reflect, and live the standard and lifestyle you see in Jesus.

Live It Strong

- Why does God want us to be like him?
- What excuses do you use that prevent you from actually living like Jesus?
- How do we "look at Jesus"?

God's Word

This is what the LORD says: "Let not the wise man boast of his wisdom or the strong man boast of his strength or the rich man boast of his riches, but let him who boasts boast about this: that he understands and knows me, that I am the LORD, who exercises kindness, justice and righteousness on earth, for in these I delight," declares the LORD. Jeremiah 9:23–24

I keep asking that the God of our Lord Jesus Christ, the glorious Father, may give you the Spirit of wisdom and revelation, so that you may know him better. I pray also that the eyes of your heart may be enlightened in order that you may know the hope to which he has called you, the riches of his glorious inheritance in the saints, and his incomparably great power for us who believe. That power is like the working of his mighty strength, which he exerted in Christ when he raised him from the dead and seated him at his right hand in the heavenly realms. Ephesians 1:17–20

What is more, I consider everything a loss compared to the surpassing greatness of knowing Christ Jesus my Lord, for whose sake I have lost all things. I consider them rubbish, that I may gain Christ. . . . I want to know Christ and the power of his resurrection and the fellowship of sharing in his sufferings. Philippians 3:8, 10

Live It

The apostle Paul was an amazing man. Imagine having the whole world figured out and then being confronted by Jesus and having your world turned upside down.

Think about what Paul surrendered when he met Jesus. He gave up a future in the Jewish religion. He gave up what was probably a significant amount of worldly possessions. He gave up his good job, popularity, and wealth to follow Jesus. I imagine Paul's surrender was like J-Lo giving up her recording contracts or LeBron James surrendering his basketball endorsements. Paul's change wasn't just spiritual, it was also financial, occupational, and as a result probably seriously emotional.

But Paul doesn't seem to see it that way. In Philippians 3:10, Paul lets us in on his motivation and passion. You'd think Paul might write, "Knowing Jesus is the perfect answer to all your problems. Don't sweat it, because Jesus will give you everything you need." You'd think that a guy like Paul would have been more comfortable with this kind of Jesus.

But Paul doesn't offer us that kind of answer, and he doesn't give us that kind of a picture of following Jesus. When you read his words in Philippians, you hear a guy who's surrendered his future to God and is following the same destiny as Jesus. Check out his words.

"I want to know Christ . . ." Based on what Paul has been saying to the church at Philippi, this isn't just Paul wanting to be friends with Jesus. His words here depict a deeper, more intimate kind of knowledge. The thing about knowing Jesus intimately is that you can't do it without having your entire world changed. That's what's happened to Paul. He encountered Jesus, he got to know Jesus, and his entire world changed. Has your world been changed?

". . . and the power of his resurrection . . ." Knowing the power of Jesus' resurrection meant that Paul didn't want Jesus to hold back. Every part of this power and his personality—Paul wants it all. What about you? Are you out to get all of him? Do you want to know all about Jesus? Do you want to understand and experience all of his power?

". . . and the fellowship of sharing in his sufferings . . ." See the contrast these words paint? Paul wasn't known for his suffering—until he met Jesus. We don't know all the details of Paul's life before he met Christ, but based on what he says about his former life, we know that he probably didn't suffer. Are you ready and willing to suffer for Christ?

". . . becoming like him in his death . . ." Suffering for Christ, taken to its ultimate extreme, results in your death. We're not talking a symbolic kind of death, and Paul isn't exaggerating here. Paul is actually offering himself to be killed for Christ. It's a huge statement from Paul. Are you willing to give your life so someone will know Christ? Could you do that?

Paul's words to the church at Philippi make us do a lot of self-examination. Considering what Paul wrote in Philippians, ask yourself the following questions: Am I willing to know Christ completely? Am I willing to know the power of Jesus' resurrection? Am I willing to know and participate in the suffering of Jesus? Am I willing to be put to death for Jesus?

Live It Strong

- What does it take to know Christ completely?
- What happens when we completely know Christ?
- How does Christ help us live for him? What does he do to help us be living examples?

Week One

God's Word

A new command I give you: Love one another. As I have loved you, so you must love one another. By this all men will know that you are my disciples, if you love one another. John 13:34–35

Now that you have purified yourselves by obeying the truth so that you have sincere love for your brothers, love one another deeply, from the heart. 1 Peter 1:22

Dear children, let us not love with words or tongue but with actions and in truth. 1 John 3:18

Live It

There's an old story about a soldier, after World War II, walking toward a bakery. As he was walking he noticed a young boy standing outside the bakery, looking hungrily through the window. The boy looked pitiful, and the soldier imagined that this young man was probably one of the thousands of children left without a family after the war. It was no wonder that this young man was staring into the bakery. If he really was an orphan, he probably hadn't eaten in days.

The soldier walked into the bakery and bought two loaves of bread. He walked outside, gave the young boy one of the loaves, patted him on the head, and kept walking.

The boy responded as the soldier walked away, "Mister, are you Jesus?"

This short story illustrates a deep spiritual truth. The more we love people, the more we resemble Jesus. The more we feed others, give of ourselves, and help the needy, the more people recognize that God is working in and through us. In essence, you are the only Jesus some people will meet. You might possibly be the only representation, the only living example of Jesus, that some unsaved person will come into contact with.

How do you live like Jesus? Do you have to walk around in sandals? Wear a robe? Should you go around trying to heal people? What does it take to be like Jesus?

A. W. Tozer, a great theologian and Christian thinker, once said, "Nearness is likeness." In other words, the closer we are to Jesus—the more we know about him—the more we are like him.

You'd like to be like Jesus? You'd like to represent our Savior to someone? Then you've got to get close to him, and you can't get close to Jesus if you're living an arm's length kind of relationship with him. A relationship with Jesus means a *relationship*. Spend time with him. Read his Word. Listen to his voice through prayer.

Being like Jesus is sometimes more involved than just getting to know everything about him, though. It's important to move beyond knowledge about Jesus and into consistently living and acting like him. Our actions have to match his actions. Our level of love for others has to match his level of love.

If you love like Jesus and live like him, someday someone may look at you, see your actions, and be introduced to Jesus. They may not know exactly what they're experiencing, and they may not know exactly who Jesus is. That's why as you're living like him you've also got to be able to speak about him.

Knowing Jesus. Living like him. Being able and ready to speak about him. It's a long list of stuff, huh?

That long list begins with your decisions. What do you do first? First, commit yourself to living like Jesus. Begin today by asking God to help you live like Jesus lived. Ask him to help you see in Scripture how Jesus lived and to give you the strength to live like Jesus. Then ask him to help you love others, serve others, and be prepared to speak about him.

Live It Strong

- How can you keep a healthy relationship with Jesus?
- What things in your life prevent you from keeping a relationship with Jesus?
- What is the first thing you should do to begin living like Christ? Do you need to ask for forgiveness? Do you need to remove some idols?

23

God's Word

And we pray this in order that you may live a life worthy of the Lord and may please him in every way: bearing fruit in every good work, growing in the knowledge of God. Colossians 1:10

Finally, brothers, we instructed you how to live in order to please God, as in fact you are living. Now we ask you and urge you in the Lord Jesus to do this more and more. . . . Make it your ambition to lead a quiet life, to mind your own business and to work with your hands, just as we told you, so that your daily life may win the respect of outsiders and so that you will not be dependent on anybody. 1 Thessalonians 4:1, 11–12

Finally, all of you, live in harmony with one another; be sympathetic, love as brothers, be compassionate and humble. . . . keeping a clear conscience, so that those who speak maliciously against your good behavior in Christ may be ashamed of their slander. 1 Peter 3:8, 16

Live It

I heard an old saying that "Some days you're the dog, some days you're the hydrant." I know that feeling really, really well.

I tend to overreact to things. On a bad day I can overreact to everything I encounter. And when I'm in the middle of one of my overreacting moments, I know I'm going way overboard, but I can't stop myself. I get so into overreacting and get so upset that I'm like a train heading for a brick wall. Too little sleep, too much frustration, and anything can get me going.

The other day I was a mess. It was an unusually stressful day, and I was in an unusually pathetic mood. Our family goes to church together, so we were all trying to get into the car and off to church. But we had all gotten up late, and we were all rushing. In our rush I stepped on some toy in the middle of the living room floor, and I overreacted. Then our youngest child wouldn't stop crying. After several minutes of hearing him cry, knowing we were late, and feeling the pain from the stupid toy I stepped on, I was *really* overreacting. I was feeling like the hydrant.

The thing that pushed me completely over the edge was really just something stupid. As I was getting stuff together, I came across a baby bottle my son had been using three or four days before. This bottle was filled with old, smelly, bacteria-filled milk. The milk had turned into runny cottage cheese. It was nasty. Well, I saw it and tried to pick it up from the top. When I did that, the top came off and the bottle dropped on the floor, splashing milk all over everything—including me.

I lost it. I kicked the toy that I'd stepped on earlier. I began to feel really sorry for myself. As I wiped the nasty milk off my pants (I didn't have time to change), I really felt like the hydrant. I was going nuts. I was overreacting.

Just as I was at my peak, talking to myself about what a bad day this was and how frustrated I was about my messy pants, I heard the following in a very high-pitched voice: "Tim Baker. Tim Baker's having a bad day. Tim Baker." Over and over. My youngest daughter was standing not too far away from me. She had been watching my little pity party. She had been watching me act like the hydrant. She was watching as I kicked the toy, yelled at the stinky milk, and generally acted stupid.

I know you don't have kids and it must sound awfully parental for you to read about how my daughter taught me something, but look, it's true. Every thing we do, every act, every word, every good thing, and every bad moment—they're all being watched. People who don't know Jesus are watching you. They're watching to see how you react to spilled milk, and they're watching to see if you're a drama queen.

Why should you be like Jesus? Because people are watching. Wouldn't you rather give them a positive impression of Jesus? Wouldn't you rather help them learn to imitate Jesus by watching you?

Live It Strong

- What things put you in a bad mood?
- When we're in a bad mood, how can God help us straighten out?
- How do our bad attitudes prevent us from imitating Jesus?

God's Word

This is to my Father's glory, that you bear much fruit, showing yourselves to be my disciples. John 15:8

For the grace of God that brings salvation has appeared to all men. It teaches us to say "No" to ungodliness and worldly passions, and to live self-controlled, upright and godly lives in this present age. Titus 2:11–12

For this very reason, make every effort to add to your faith goodness; and to goodness, knowledge; and to knowledge, self-control; and to self-control, perseverance; and to perseverance, godliness; and to godliness, brotherly kindness; and to brotherly kindness, love. For if you possess these qualities in increasing measure, they will keep you from being ineffective and unproductive in your knowledge of our Lord Jesus Christ. 2 Peter 1:5–8

Live It

Jeff has always been a different kind of kid. You've known him since you were in kindergarten, but you really don't hang out with him except at church. Jeff has a different take on everything, including Bible stuff. He seems to take it so seriously. How seriously? At Bible study, Jeff is just *too* into the whole thing. He brings a stack of colored markers and spends the entire time marking up his Bible. Every little thing your youth pastor says, Jeff underlines something in his Bible or writes in the margin. Jeff always leads in prayer, and he prays for a looooonnggg time. He's just . . . well . . . he's just too religious. It's getting on your nerves a bit.

This week, though, Jeff went too far. After a Bible study on being Christlike, Jeff was unusually quiet. He didn't talk much and wouldn't respond to anyone who tried talking to him. After the final prayer (he didn't even pray one of his long, drawn out ones tonight) Jeff left quietly without saying good-bye. The rest of the group sat commenting about Jeff and wondering if maybe he'd grown up a bit.

But he hadn't changed at all. The next day at school you noticed Jeff in the lunchroom. He was wearing what looked like an old bedsheet tied at his waist with a long piece of rope. You couldn't believe it, so you just stood there and watched. Should you go over and talk to him? Maybe you should sit somewhere else. Just as you were about to go talk to him, Jeff stood on a chair and began reading very loudly out of the Book of Revelation.

Before long your pity for Jeff took over, and you went and pulled him off the chair.

"Jeff, what are you doing? You look completely stupid!"

Jeff looked at you like *you* were stupid. "Weren't you listening at Bible study last night? Didn't you hear about how we're supposed to be like Christ? I'm just doing what we talked about last night. Were you just not listening? Or don't you care about being like Jesus?"

This was weird—even for Jeff. You decided to walk away and let him cool down. It's been three weeks, and you haven't talked to him since.

Live It Strong

- How would you help Jeff understand that he's confused about what it means to be like Christ?
- What Scriptures would you show Jeff to help him see the life-style Jesus expects from his followers?
- What would you say to Jeff to help him realistically live like Jesus?

God's Word

As for God, his way is perfect; the word of the LORD is flawless. He is a shield for all who take refuge in him. Psalm 18:30

Jesus answered, "I am the way and the truth and the life. No one comes to the Father except through me. If you really knew me, you would know my Father as well. From now on, you do know him and have seen him." John 14:6–7

Let us fix our eyes on Jesus, the author and perfecter of our faith, who for the joy set before him endured the cross, scorning its shame, and sat down at the right hand of the throne of God. Hebrews 12:2

Live It

Imitating Jesus might sound kind of weird. You can't see him. He's not physically standing right next to you. You don't have a video of him and his actions in the world. So imitating Jesus isn't the easiest thing to do. How can you learn more about imitating and being like Jesus? Try this.

Ask a friend to help you. Explain to your friend that you'd like him to stand still, facing you, and slowly move his hands. As he moves his hands, you'll move yours as a mirror image of them. When you get better at imitating his hand movements, you can ask your friend to add facial and body movements also.

Tell your friend to begin, and do your best to imitate his actions exactly. Pay attention to his face, hands, and body, and do exactly what he does.

So how is this like imitating Jesus?

First of all, you're staring at your friend and imitating him. In the same way, when you stare at Jesus by knowing his actions and knowing his life, you can better imitate his actions. How can you imitate someone you're not watching? You can't.

Second, you're moving like your friend is moving. Imitating your friend involves doing exactly what he's doing. If he does something, you do it. If he doesn't, you don't. Imitating Jesus involves this same thing—doing what he does.

Being like Jesus is like imitating your best friend in this exercise. You watch so closely that you know the movements of your friend and you do exactly what he does. How do you imitate Jesus? You watch and imitate. No frills. There's no special sauce you dump on yourself, and there's no secret potion you take. You watch and imitate.

What about you? Do you imitate Jesus? You've got to watch Jesus. Get to know him through reading the Gospels. Get to know others' reactions to him through reading the New Testament letters. Do everything you can to get to know Jesus so that you can be his perfect imitator.

Live It Strong

- What have you learned about imitating Jesus from this activity?
- Using what you've learned from this illustration, how would you explain how to imitate Jesus to your best friend?
- How can you apply what you've learned about imitating Jesus from this illustration and from Scripture to your life?

WHY
IS
PRAYER
SO IMPORTANT?

God's Word

For he will command his angels concerning you to guard you in all your ways. Psalm 91:11

I want men everywhere to lift up holy hands in prayer, without anger or disputing. 1 Timothy 2:8

Let us then approach the throne of grace with confidence, so that we may receive mercy and find grace to help us in our time of need. Hebrews 4:16

Live It

Lying there in the dark, you begin to pray, like you do every night just before you drift off to sleep. You begin to lay out your requests. One by one, you work through your list. Paul's college scholarship. Lacey's dog. As each request leaves your lips, you slowly begin to drift into dreamland. Slowly your body relaxes, your mind lets go, and you fall to sleep. Actively praying. Actively resting before God.

On the other side, no one is sleeping. There are beings like you've never seen with human eyes. They're listening to you, and they're listening to God. As you pray, they move. As God commands, things begin to change. Situations get worked out. Limbs are healed. Futures are restored. Lives are mended.

Prayer is an unusual thing. Ever thought about it? It's our connection to God. It's our mode of confession. Prayer is our way of telling God our hopes and dreams. If it's true that the cornerstone of every good relationship is communication, then prayer is an essential element in our relationship with God.

What happens when you pray? Are your prayers a connection to an unseen world where God is working all the time for your happiness and health? Are there angels working to straighten your life out? Maybe there's a communication chain—an angel who listens to you when you pray, then passes your requests on to a senior angel, who passes it up the chain to God. And then God, in his infinite wisdom and kindness, works to meet the request you've laid out.

Why Is Prayer
So Important?

Or maybe we're not supposed to know anything about prayer. Maybe the act of praying and the hows and whys of prayer are *supposed* to be a secret.

This week we're going to discover what makes prayer so important. No deep theology here. Nothing over your head. This week we're tackling the simple act of prayer. Make sure you take time to actually pray this week. Keep track of what you're praying about and the answers that God brings.

Live It Strong

- Why is prayer important?
- What makes prayer difficult for you?
- What can you do this week to help you pray more often?

God's Word

And pray in the Spirit on all occasions with all kinds of prayers and requests. With this in mind, be alert and always keep on praying for all the saints. Ephesians 6:18

Do not be anxious about anything, but in everything, by prayer and petition, with thanksgiving, present your requests to God. Philippians 4:6

This, then, is how you should pray: "Our Father in heaven, hallowed be your name, your kingdom come, your will be done on earth as it is in heaven. Give us today our daily bread. Forgive us our debts, as we also have forgiven our debtors. And lead us not into temptation, but deliver us from the evil one." Matthew 6:9–13

Live It

If you're like me, you've struggled with the "right way" to pray. Since prayer is talking to God, you want to make sure that you're using the right words and saying the right things. I've worried that I wasn't talking to God right, and I've searched for and asked people about the best way to address God.

The best way to learn about how to talk to God is to look at the life of Jesus. Check out Matthew 6:9–13. Jesus is in the middle of the Sermon on the Mount, which was a talk Jesus gave to a crowd of people. As he talks about a variety of topics, Jesus gets on the subject of prayer and gives a very interesting, easy format for talking to God. Jesus' format helps us remember key ideas in prayer.

"Our Father in heaven, hallowed be your name . . ."

Addressing God begins with recognizing who God is and what he is like. This is the cool part of prayer: recognizing God and telling him how cool we think he is. This acknowledgment of God's personality is extremely important. It reminds us who we're talking to and what this almighty being can do.

". . . your kingdom come, your will be done on earth as it is in heaven. . . ."

God's will is unstoppable, but you can still tell him that you'd like to know it and you're willing to follow it.

". . . Give us today our daily bread. . . ."

Have you ever thought about how totally okay it is to ask God for things? God loves it when his children turn to him and ask for stuff. It's okay to ask God for food, clothes, and other necessities.

". . . Forgive us our debts, as we also have forgiven our debtors. . . ."

Forgiveness is a two-way street. God will forgive us as long as we ask for his forgiveness. And just as we're forgiven, we need to forgive others. Prayer offers us access to God and the opportunity to receive forgiveness.

". . . And lead us not into temptation, but deliver us from the evil one."

A cornerstone of prayer is asking God to protect us for help with temptation. As we walk this earth as followers of God, it's too easy to give up and give in to sin.

So what do you do with Jesus' formula? How do you put what Jesus recommends into practice in your life?

It's actually not that difficult. If you trim down and translate Jesus' formula, what you get is an awesomely easy way to pray, something like this:

1. *Begin with praise.* Remember to tell God what you love about him.
2. *Tell God your needs.* God loves to provide for every need we have. Telling God what your needs are is an important part of your communication with him, a lot like a child telling her parents what her needs are.
3. *Ask God for forgiveness.* Part of a relationship is asking forgiveness.
4. *Ask God for protection.* God loves to protect his children. And when you ask God for protection you're asking him to keep you safe like a parent.

Live It Strong

- Why is prayer an important part of your relationship with God?
- What makes praying difficult for you?
- What's the best way to follow Jesus' directions for prayer?

God's Word

Give ear to my words, O LORD, consider my sighing. Listen to my cry for help, my King and my God, for to you I pray. Psalm 5:1–2

Then he said to them, "My soul is overwhelmed with sorrow to the point of death. Stay here and keep watch with me." Going a little farther, he fell with his face to the ground and prayed, "My Father, if it is possible, may this cup be taken from me. Yet not as I will, but as you will." Matthew 26:38–39

In the same way, the Spirit helps us in our weakness. We do not know what we ought to pray for, but the Spirit himself intercedes for us with groans that words cannot express. And he who searches our hearts knows the mind of the Spirit, because the Spirit intercedes for the saints in accordance with God's will. Romans 8:26–27

Live It

Jesus' explanation of the correct way to pray helps us know the right format, order, and tone with which we are supposed to address God. Yesterday's devotion was about the right format—the right words and the right way to address God.

But Jesus doesn't always use the "right format" to talk to God. In fact, when you read his prayer in the Garden of Gethsemane (Matthew 26:36–46), you realize that the "format" in what's been called "the Lord's Prayer" (Matthew 6:9–13) is just a suggestion because in the Garden, Jesus demonstrates the other side of prayer: *passion.*

As he's about to be betrayed by someone he loves, be arrested, and begin a long night of trials and beatings which will ultimately end with his death, Jesus prays with passion and honesty. When you read Matthew 26:36–46, you're reading about Jesus' last moments as a free man. In these important moments, Jesus shows us the necessity of prayer in desperate times.

Read Jesus' prayer in the Garden. What is important about Jesus' prayer?

Jesus prays. I know what you're thinking—*too obvious.* I don't think so, because I don't think that we always automatically think to pray. If you're like me, praying is often the last thing you do when you're upset. I often react badly or get angry when I'm facing a tough situation. To see Jesus praying as he's facing arrest, beatings, and crucifixion is a pretty amazing thing.

Jesus is honest. I'm not sure I could be this honest with God. At this point Jesus must know that the weight of everyone's sin will be on his shoulders. We know that he knows that something bad is coming because he asks God to prevent what's coming up from happening (unless it's part of his plan). Jesus' honesty is motivating, isn't it? Since Jesus was honest, we can be honest with God too.

Jesus is committed. Through this prayer you see Jesus' commitment. And it's not just a commitment to God or to the disciples. You see Jesus' commitment to his identity as the crucified lamb. In some way our commitment ought to mirror Jesus' commitment.

Have you ever been desperate? Have you ever wanted to be honest with God but felt like you weren't sure if that was okay? Have you ever wanted to tell God something but been afraid that he'd get mad at you for what you said?

Jesus shows us that it's okay to pray when we feel desperate. His actions help us see that it's even okay to question God's plan—it's okay to ask God why. As long as we're willing to listen to God's answer and accept it, asking why and saying we wonder about God's plan is okay.

That's what Jesus does. And that's what we can do too.

Yeah, prayer can be a formula. And when you're not sure how to pray, following a formula for prayer can be a great way to talk to God. But when you're hurting or feeling like you don't know God's plan, let your passion take over. Let your heart speak. It's okay to ask God why, and it's okay to tell him that you don't understand. Jesus did that, and it's okay for you to do that too.

Live It Strong

- Why is it difficult to pray when you're hurting?
- How does God help us when we don't know how to pray?
- Is it always okay to be completely honest with God? Are there some things that you shouldn't say to God?

God's Word

Before they call I will answer; while they are still speaking I will hear. Isaiah 65:24

Therefore I tell you, whatever you ask for in prayer, believe that you have received it, and it will be yours. And when you stand praying, if you hold anything against anyone, forgive him, so that your Father in heaven may forgive you your sins. Mark 11:24–25

In the same way, the Spirit helps us in our weakness. We do not know what we ought to pray for, but the Spirit himself intercedes for us with groans that words cannot express. Romans 8:26

Live It

Have you ever been attacked? I don't mean has anyone ever walked up to you and beat you with a PlayStation 2 controller. I mean have you ever been told off? Has it ever seemed like someone in your life was out to get you? Have you had days when it seemed like everything they did was done to hurt you, like they didn't live for anything else but to see you in serious emotional pain?

I always thought that when I was being attacked by people or felt attacked by a bad situation, I was alone. I can remember many times in my life when I felt like I was being abused beyond belief. Sometimes it was a best friend who decided that we were actually enemies and that he would make sure all our friends liked him and hated me. Other times it seemed like someone that I didn't really even know was just out to get me.

When life is rotten, that's when you pray, right? If you did a survey I bet you'd find that more people pray when their lives are awful than pray when their lives are going great. We tend to talk to God when we're desperate and push him aside and ignore him when we're feeling great. But what happens when you pray and it feels like your prayers are just bouncing off the ceiling? How do you keep praying when you feel rotten and feel like God can't hear you?

Romans 8:26 gives the answer. When we feel so rotten and abused that we can't pray or don't know how to pray, the Holy Spirit prays for us. We don't know what he says for us, but we're promised that he'll talk to God on our behalf.

That means when you feel like you can't pray, you can at least pray a few words and know that the Holy Spirit will take your hurt to God. When you feel so attacked that you don't know what to say to God, say something out loud. Yell at the wall, and let the Holy Spirit take your anger to God.

Live It Strong

- Why is praying when we're hurting so important?
- When have you felt like you couldn't pray? What happened?
- What happens if we don't pray when we're hurting?

God's Word

And when you pray, do not be like the hypocrites, for they love to pray standing in the synagogues and on the street corners to be seen by men. I tell you the truth, they have received their reward in full. But when you pray, go into your room, close the door and pray to your Father, who is unseen. Then your Father, who sees what is done in secret, will reward you. And when you pray, do not keep on babbling like pagans, for they think they will be heard because of their many words. Matthew 6:5–7

Now to him who is able to do immeasurably more than all we ask or imagine, according to his power that is at work within us, to him be glory in the church and in Christ Jesus throughout all generations, for ever and ever! Amen. Ephesians 3:20–21

Let us then approach the throne of grace with confidence, so that we may receive mercy and find grace to help us in our time of need. Hebrews 4:16

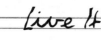

Live It

In the lunchroom, you and your friends talk like real people. *Real* people! Not like you talk to your teachers, or to your parents, or even to your youth pastor. You talk like real people, don't you? You talk about real stuff. You talk about the real problems you're having, not the surface stuff you tell others.

Take just a minute and think about the last time you sat around the lunch table with your friends. What kind of stuff did you talk about? What issues? *How* did you talk to each other? What kind of language did you use? Did you talk to each other like . . .

"Dearesteth friendeth. Thou hast chosen thyself garments befitting the brightest side of thy personality."

40

No. Did you talk to each other like . . .

"My daddy says that when I grow up, I can still play with dolls. My daddy said that my shoes are faster than yours. Next year, when Santa comes, my mommy says that I'll get a new dollhouse. My birthday is next week, and I'm going to have pony rides and rainbow cotton candy."

No, I bet you didn't talk to each other like you were four-year-olds. Okay, did you talk like . . .

"Yo, dude . . . 'sup. This grub is whack. Word up, yo, I wouldn't feed this munch to my worst hater."

I bet you didn't talk to each other like that either. I bet you talked like you normally do, like any students sitting around a table eating. I bet you talked about normal stuff, too, not about ponies or food or whatever.

Sometimes when we talk to God, we feel like we have to use certain language or a special group of words. We feel like God won't listen to us or can't hear us unless we use special language or talk like a child or whatever. Sometimes when I listen to people pray, I can't help wondering what God thinks about the way they're praying and the kind of language they're using. I wonder how God feels about the way we pray. I wonder what he thinks about the kind of language we use when we tell him about our concerns or ask him for help.

Next time you pray imagine that you're sitting at the lunch table talking to your best friend. Imagine that you're talking about normal stuff like school or your last conversation with your crush. Imagine that you're involved in a normal conversation with your best friend—someone who loves you and wants the best for you.

Live It Strong

- How do you talk to God? Do you talk like your grandfather? Like a baby?
- Do you think God cares how we talk to him? Why?
- Why is it important to talk to God like he's right there with you, like at a lunch table?

God's Word

And pray in the Spirit on all occasions with all kinds of prayers and requests. With this in mind, be alert and always keep on praying for all the saints. Ephesians 6:18

Therefore confess your sins to each other and pray for each other so that you may be healed. The prayer of a righteous man is powerful and effective. James 5:16

The end of all things is near. Therefore be clear minded and self-controlled so that you can pray. Above all, love each other deeply, because love covers over a multitude of sins. 1 Peter 4:7–8

Live It

Brent is the most pessimistic person you've ever met. He can't stand most of the polite sayings that people usually spew out. For example, the other day you passed Brent in the hall and tossed a simple "How's it going, man?" at him. Brent wasn't having that, and he let you know it. He stopped you right there in the hall to point out your insincerity.

"You don't care a bit about how I'm doing. You don't really want to know. You're just being polite. I'm tired of people acting like they care." Brent went on and on. His unending rambling about the hypocrisy of Christians made you tired.

That's why you're not surprised about what happened yesterday in Sunday school. Your youth pastor was asking for prayer requests. As each person mentioned a praise or a need, she wrote it down to pass on to the entire church. After several people mentioned their needs, Brent chimed in with a request about getting a job for the summer. He's planning on going with some friends next year on a graduation trip to Norway, and wants to begin saving for the trip. Brent looks around the room as he shares, and seems intent on being as serious as possible.

After he's finished talking, your youth pastor says, "Alright, who will take his request before the Lord." Sandy piped up and said she'd pray for it. And for some reason this sets Brent off. Brent went into a tirade about how Sandy needed to take his request seriously. When Sandy gave him a kind of annoyed look, Brent took his tirade to the next level. And, just like he laid into you about not caring about him, he lit into Sandy about not taking his prayer request seriously.

"This is important to me," Brent began, "and I don't need you to mention this to God with that kind of attitude. This is serious. Prayer is serious. Why doesn't someone else who takes prayer seriously pray about this for me. I don't need Sandy's attitude."

The room was silent. Everyone just stared at Brent with their mouths open. Before long, Sandy started to cry. Your youth pastor went over to Sandy and walked her out of the room. You want to say something to Brent and the rest of the room and get a discussion going about prayer and Brent's actions, but you're not exactly sure how you should get it started.

Live It Strong

- How would you help Brent understand how his words hurt Sandy?
- What should the youth pastor do in this situation?
- What would you say to Brent to help him understand the benefits of letting others pray for us?

God's Word

I love the LORD, for he heard my voice; he heard my cry for mercy. Because he turned his ear to me, I will call on him as long as I live. Psalm 116:1–2

Ask and it will be given to you; seek and you will find; knock and the door will be opened to you. For everyone who asks receives; he who seeks finds; and to him who knocks, the door will be opened. Matthew 7:7–8

Devote yourselves to prayer, being watchful and thankful. Colossians 4:2

Live It

When you pray, what do you notice happening? Have you ever seen the effects of prayer? Have you ever noticed something happening when you pray? Ever seen God's hand moving after one of your requests? Ever heard God's voice after you prayed, offering you an answer or promising to give you what you asked for?

I haven't. And that can be one of the most frustrating aspects of prayer—always praying, not always hearing a response.

How can you get a better understanding of the process of prayer? What physical thing demonstrates the process of prayer?

Try this.

On a windy day, go sit outside. I don't mean just sit for a minute and then go back inside, I mean sit outside for a while. While you're outside, notice the effects that wind has on the world around you. Do you see how the wind affects the trees and the grass?

Once you've observed this for a while, go get a balloon. Blow it up and write a prayer request on the balloon (something you don't mind other people reading, because you might not get the balloon back). Take it back outside and let it go into the wind.

What do you notice?

If it's a really windy day, the balloon will get taken up into the sky. It will be tossed here and there but eventually make it up pretty high. What's taking the balloon up? What's pushing it around? The wind. You can't see the wind, but you can see the effects of the wind.

This is a great picture of prayer. Like the wind, prayer can't actually be seen, but you can see the effects of it and know that it's working. Even though you can't see prayer, the effects of communication with God can radically change you and affect every problem you face.

Live It Strong

- What have you learned about prayer from this activity?
- Using what you've learned from this illustration, how would you explain prayer to your best friend?
- How can you apply what you've learned about prayer from this illustration and from Scripture to your life?

WHY
SHOULD I HAVE
COURAGE?

God's Word

And you, son of man, do not be afraid of them or their words. Do not be afraid, though briers and thorns are all around you and you live among scorpions. Do not be afraid of what they say or terrified by them, though they are a rebellious house. Ezekiel 2:6

Be on your guard; stand firm in the faith; be men of courage; be strong. 1 Corinthians 16:13

Whatever happens, conduct yourselves in a manner worthy of the gospel of Christ. Then, whether I come and see you or only hear about you in my absence, I will know that you stand firm in one spirit, contending as one man for the faith of the gospel without being frightened in any way by those who oppose you. This is a sign to them that they will be destroyed, but that you will be saved—and that by God. Philippians 1:27–28

Live It

You stand on the battlefield, sword in hand, shield on your forearm.

Sweat beads on your forehead as you survey the battlefield. To your left are friends who are trying to lead you away from God. On your right are bad habits. Directly behind you is an army of demons who are pushing you into failure and defeat. And directly in front of you are sins that have been chasing you for months.

You're trapped. You look out and wonder if this is a fight you can win. Losing to these enemies could reshape the rest of your life. Defeating them won't be easy. You'll have to stand firm and fight. But this is your life. Not someone else's problem. Not another person's sins. This is *your* fight.

What do you need right now? Courage.

Being willing to fight won't be enough. Having the ability to fight won't be enough either. You've got to actually do it. You've got to actually face them.

What is courage? Is it training? Is courage the ability to beat your opponent? Is courage the willingness to face the opponent no matter how powerful it is or how scary it appears?

How would you define courage? Write a definition here:

_____

_____

_____

_____

Courage is the willingness to stand your ground. Courage doesn't mean you're the best trained. It doesn't necessarily mean that you're better than your opponents. It simply means that you'll stand up to them—whatever they are.

You see, some people never stand. Even though they have the ability, the weapons, and even a little desire, they never stand. They never use their courage.

This week is about you and your courage. Like many people, you have the tools to defend yourself. But do you have the desire? Are you willing to stand against the things that hinder your walk with God? Are you willing to defend your relationship with him?

This is your week to flex your courage. Get to it.

Live It Strong

- Why is courage an important part of life for Christians?
- What things in your life prevent you from having courage?
- What situations can you use your courage in during this week that will help you build it and stand up for God?

God's Word

But you will receive power when the Holy Spirit comes on you; and you will be my witnesses in Jerusalem, and in all Judea and Samaria, and to the ends of the earth. Acts 1:8

The following night the Lord stood near Paul and said, "Take courage! As you have testified about me in Jerusalem, so you must also testify in Rome." Acts 23:11

So we say with confidence, "The Lord is my helper; I will not be afraid. What can man do to me?" Hebrews 13:6

Live It

I've never met people more courageous than the people I was with for one of my first witnessing experiences.

I was working in a church, ministering to college students, and these students were interested in talking to others about their faith. They were adamant about telling others about what they believed. They asked me to go with them. They didn't want me to talk to people for them, and they really didn't even need me. But I went anyway.

These students could have picked any kind of neighborhood. They could have picked a neighborhood where the surroundings weren't as scary and the streets were safer. But they didn't. They chose an area of the city that was notorious for being rough, mean, and generally unkind to people like these students. These guys were typical computer nerd types. They looked kinda uncool, and they weren't that comfortable talking to new people. But they wanted to go witness, and I didn't feel right about trying to stop them.

They chose to start at an extremely busy gas station on a Friday night. As we drove up, we all commented on how packed the store attached to the gas station was. There were people everywhere hanging out and talking. As we got out of the car, the four guys I was with scattered like they had a plan. Two went walking down one street well known for being filled with drug dealers. The other two went walking down another street that was equally rough. They left me standing there. I was nervous.

So I stood there. I was supposed to witness to people, but I didn't. I was supposed to get to know people, but I didn't. I just stood there like a scared pastor. People walked by and stared at me. I was obviously out of place wearing a pair of dress pants and a tie while I was surrounded by homeless guys and drug pushers. I just stood there.

About an hour later, the guys I went with showed up. They had equally bad results. Turns out they just wandered the neighborhoods. They hadn't talked to one person. They didn't tell anyone about Jesus. All of us felt like complete failures.

Truth is, we were.

I learned a lot about courage that night. You can't go and do *half* of God's will just because you're feeling courageous at the start. Even when we know God's called us or when we feel bold and courageous, it's completely possible for us to *try* to do something awesome for God but fail because our courage didn't carry through. But it doesn't do any good to follow God halfway.

That night I learned that when God gives you the courage to go somewhere dangerous, he also gives you the ability to do what he calls you to do. God didn't give me courage to stand outside the store on the rough side of town; God gave me courage to *witness* for him, but my weakness held me back. My weakness prevented me from actually doing what God asked.

That's a hard lesson to learn. We so often pray for courage, and God gives it to us. But then we often fail to follow through using the courage we've been given.

Live It Strong

- When have you felt courageous but then caved?
- How do you think God responds to us when we mess up like this?
- What should we do when we fail at something God wants us to do?

51

God's Word

Then Moses summoned Joshua and said to him in the presence of all Israel, "Be strong and courageous, for you must go with this people into the land that the LORD swore to their forefathers to give them, and you must divide it among them as their inheritance. The LORD himself goes before you and will be with you; he will never leave you nor forsake you. Do not be afraid; do not be discouraged." Deuteronomy 31:7–8

Be strong and courageous, because you will lead these people to inherit the land I swore to their forefathers to give them. Be strong and very courageous. Be careful to obey all the law my servant Moses gave you; do not turn from it to the right or to the left, that you may be successful wherever you go. Joshua 1:6–7

When the time drew near for David to die, he gave a charge to Solomon his son. "I am about to go the way of all the earth," he said. "So be strong, show yourself a man, and observe what the LORD your God requires: Walk in his ways, and keep his decrees and commands, his laws and requirements, as written in the Law of Moses, so that you may prosper in all you do and wherever you go." 1 Kings 2:1–3

Live It

It's almost impossible to fill the shoes of an important, influential leader. It's one thing to take on someone's job like being a dishwasher or mowing lawns. Those are necessary jobs, but they're not that difficult to imitate.

But what if you had to imitate the actions and leadership of a great leader? What if you were recruited to take over the leadership of your school, or maybe of a local restaurant? Those are big jobs.

Joshua grew up to be a leader under the watchful eye of Moses. He was selected to learn leadership from Moses and grew up learning how to lead thousands of people. When Moses dealt with the Israelites, Joshua was watching. When Moses had to make tough leadership decisions, Joshua was watching. As God directed Moses, Moses directed Joshua.

Why Should I
Have Courage?

So when Moses was about to die and give up his leadership of the Israelites, he followed God's leading and passed the leadership on to Joshua. And even though Moses had trained Joshua, even though Joshua had been groomed for the position, and even though Joshua had been handpicked by God, Moses gives Joshua some interesting advice. You can find his advice in Deuteronomy 31:7–8. Take a minute to read that passage.

Did you see Moses' advice? Words like "be strong" and "courageous" rang in my head when I read that passage. Joshua had the training and experience to succeed Moses. He obviously had the power, and he had God's hand on him too. So why did he also need courage? What did courage give Joshua that all those other things didn't give him?

You can't know the answer to that without knowing the rest of Joshua's history as the leader of the Israelites. When you read on in the book of Joshua, you realize why Joshua needed courage. Joshua led the Israelites to conquer great nations of people. Remember the battle of Jericho (Joshua 5:13–6:27)? Have you ever read about the wars the Israelites faced as they entered the land God gave them? (Check out Joshua 8:1–29 for a good example.) How about the job Joshua had dividing up the promised land to the Israelites (Joshua 18)? Those are moments that watching your leader doesn't prepare you for. Those are tough leadership jobs that only having huge courage prepares you for. You can have the training and the schooling and even the right trainer. But if you don't have the courage to do it, all the training doesn't mean anything.

Do you have courage? That's what it takes, you know. Yeah, you need someone to teach you what to do. You need someone to show you the right way. But they can't do it for you, and they can't make you use your courage. You have to listen to God and obey what he's asking you to do. Then you have to have the courage to do it.

live It Strong

- What part of Joshua's life was most courageous?
- How does courage help us face tough challenges?
- How difficult is it to live courageously for God as a teenager? Why?

God's Word

For you created my inmost being; you knit me together in my mother's womb. I praise you because I am fearfully and wonderfully made; your works are wonderful, I know that full well. . . . How precious to me are your thoughts, O God! How vast is the sum of them! Psalm 139: 13–14, 17

Fear of man will prove to be a snare, but whoever trusts in the LORD is kept safe. Proverbs 29:25

I, even I, am he who comforts you. Who are you that you fear mortal men, the sons of men, who are but grass, that you forget the LORD your Maker, who stretched out the heavens and laid the foundations of the earth, that you live in constant terror every day because of the wrath of the oppressor, who is bent on destruction? For where is the wrath of the oppressor? Isaiah 51:12–13

Live It

Have you ever met a human punching bag? You know the kind of person I'm talking about. The kind of person who doesn't stand up for himself. The kind of person who is the butt of all the jokes. The oddball kind of person who's easy to just forget about until you need someone to be negative about.

I know a human punching bag.

I know this guy who's probably a lot like the punching bag you know. This guy has perfected the art of apologizing for everything. Not that he's done anything wrong or anything. Tell him you've had a bad day and he'll say "I'm sorry" like your bad day was his fault.

But this easily slap-able, always-made-fun-of guy doesn't stop at apologizing for everything. He's also the least confident student I've ever met. Even though he studies and works hard at getting good grades, every time he gets an A he says, "But that test was easy," or "The teacher was just giving me a break." See? No confidence.

It gets worse. This guy is teased all the time, and honestly, he makes it really easy. He carries himself like he ought to be teased. His weird hairline (too high in the front, too high in the back) makes him an easy target for toupee jokes. His awkward, slumped walk makes an obvious target for jokes about a caveman walk.

I often watch this guy and wonder who is more lacking in courage—him or the people who tease him. When someone apologizes for every one of his actions and makes fun of his own intelligence, you've got to wonder if he just wants to be teased. Is that his only identity—the stupid, funny-walking person who would rather be made fun of than be invisible?

Those of us who walk around this planet ought to remember my friend, the human punching bag. Every time you make fun of yourself, you're expressing a lack of the courage to accept who God made you to be and what you've accomplished. Every time you allow others to put you down, you're allowing people to lessen the importance God gave us.

You weren't made to be punched. You weren't created to get picked on. You weren't formed and fashioned in your mother's womb so that later you could stand up and say, "Look how stupid I am!"

No. You were created to walk with your head up. You were formed to glorify God. Walking around without courage doesn't glorify God. Courage is the ability to walk, speak, and act like you know you're God's creation. Because you are God's creation, courage lets you tell teasers to be quiet, and it allows you to ignore the lies that try to get in your head to tell you you're worthless.

Human punching bags? Nah. Not us.

Walk with your head up. Today you may face something enormously difficult. Face it with the courage only God's good creation can face it with.

Live It Strong

- What makes you feel like a human punching bag?
- What's the difference between thinking too much of yourself and having a healthy view of yourself?
- What does God think about us when we put ourselves down?

God's Word

O LORD, the hope of Israel, all who forsake you will be put to shame. Those who turn away from you will be written in the dust because they have forsaken the LORD, the spring of living water. Jeremiah 17:13

Then one of the Twelve—the one called Judas Iscariot—went to the chief priests and asked, "What are you willing to give me if I hand him over to you?" So they counted out for him thirty silver coins. From then on Judas watched for an opportunity to hand him over. Matthew 26:14–15

When Judas, who had betrayed him, saw that Jesus was condemned, he was seized with remorse and returned the thirty silver coins to the chief priests and the elders. "I have sinned," he said, "for I have betrayed innocent blood." "What is that to us?" they replied. "That's your responsibility." So Judas threw the money into the temple and left. Then he went away and hanged himself. Matthew 27:3–5

Live It

No one likes a coward. I can't imagine any society or any group that would honor a coward, can you? How would you define a coward? No spine? Unable to stand up for his convictions? Cowards betray themselves and often the people they hang with.

Remember Judas? I have this theory about Judas. I'm not sure you'll agree with me, but just listen for a sec. I think that Judas was the biggest coward recorded in Scripture. Here's why I think that.

First, Judas's cowardly spirit oozed into the lives of others. Judas acting as a coward led to Jesus' death. Judas was tempted to betray Jesus and when he was offered a price seemed ready and willing to give Jesus up to the authorities. Judas demonstrates the lengths a coward will go to for a buck.

Second, Judas killed himself because he was full of grief over betraying Jesus. If betraying Jesus wasn't bad enough, Judas then chose to betray himself because he was unwilling to face others and unable to face what he had done.

Judas had been in the presence of Jesus. He'd experienced some major miracles. He'd seen the Savior at work teaching and refining the Old Testament laws. Judas knew the change in his own heart, and if that wasn't enough, he had a front row seat for major ministry. That's why I think he's a coward. Even with all of that, he still chose to betray Jesus.

Judas. What a coward. Imagine having access to the Messiah and blowing it. Imagine having the chance to have a major impact on the world and instead choosing to kill yourself. What a freak.

It's easy to point our fingers at Judas, isn't it? It's easy to point out all the things he should have known and all the things he gave up when he betrayed Jesus and killed himself. But don't we do the same thing? Haven't we all had our "Judas moments"?

I have. I've had moments in my walk with Christ that I'd rather forget, times when I praised God with my mouth and then just hours later betrayed him. Most of us have to admit that we've ignored or betrayed Jesus with the same passion that Judas expressed. That's the tough thing about having the courage to follow Christ with everything you are. Things compete daily for your love and attention. These things don't care that you're trying to focus on Christ.

Have you had a Judas moment? Ever betrayed Jesus? I hope not. But if you have, you can be assured that Jesus understands and he forgives you. Have the courage today to honestly look at your walk with Christ. Do you betray Jesus just by having certain habits? Do you have attitudes that reveal you live a lifestyle different than the one Jesus wants you to live?

Cowards give in and betray. Cowards don't have the courage to face their mistakes. Are you a coward, or do you have the courage to stand up for Christ?

Live It Strong

- What are some ways we betray Jesus?
- Why does it take courage to stand up for Jesus?
- What things in your life betray Jesus? What attitudes do you have that go against Jesus' character? What things do you do that go against the teachings of Jesus?

God's Word

Starting a quarrel is like breaching a dam; so drop the matter before a dispute breaks out. . . . A friend loves at all times, and a brother is born for adversity. Proverbs 17:14, 17

If you keep on biting and devouring each other, watch out or you will be destroyed by each other. Galatians 5:15

Don't have anything to do with foolish and stupid arguments, because you know they produce quarrels. And the Lord's servant must not quarrel; instead, he must be kind to everyone, able to teach, not resentful. 2 Timothy 2:23–24

Live It

It's been weeks since you've talked. He started it. It wasn't your fault that you missed the shot, but he thought it was. In practice the day after the game, he kept picking at you about missing it, and the fight escalated from there.

When Ryan wouldn't stop lecturing about the missed shot, you got into it. You hit back with a verbal abuse that's not really typical of you. But when your back is against the wall, you'll say anything to defend yourself.

Good fights take a lot of energy. And by the time both of you were finished verbally taking each other apart, you were too tired to hit. But you really didn't even need to use your fists. You'd beaten him with awful words about his parents' divorce, the girl that dumped him, and his bad acne problem. When the fight was over, you used the only energy you had left to walk away.

You've stayed away from him ever since. You haven't even talked to him. Since then you've had this weird sick feeling in your stomach. Nothing feels right.

The worst part about it is that the two of you are lab partners in Biology, and you sit next to each other in French. Just as much as friendship ties you together with someone, a good fight completely repels you. Biology and French have been excruciating.

You miss your best friend. Yeah, you're a guy, and it's kind of girly to admit it—but you're lonely.

So you've got options. You can approach Ryan and apologize, or you can just keep on with the way things are post-fight.

It takes so much courage to apologize, doesn't it? You've got to put yourself on the line and give up your desires and emotions for the sake of a relationship with your best friend.

It takes courage, doesn't it?

Live It Strong

- What does the Bible tell you to do in this situation?
- How would you apologize to Ryan?
- What might prevent you from having the courage to talk to Ryan?

God's Word

Do not be afraid of them or terrified by them, though they are a rebellious house. Ezekiel 3:9

Be on your guard; stand firm in the faith; be men of courage; be strong. 1 Corinthians 16:13

For God did not give us a spirit of timidity, but a spirit of power, of love and of self-discipline. 2 Timothy 1:7

Live It

Courage is the ability to stand up despite a variety of things that try to push you down. One way we stand up is physically, and you might have difficulty physically standing. If you do, or know someone who does, then you know the courage it takes to face the challenges that each day brings. But standing up can also be metaphorical. Some of us need courage every day to stand against tough emotions and difficult people. Courage takes many forms.

All of us have something that we lack courage for. Some of us face really mean teachers every day, and we wish that we had the courage to be honest with them. Others of us have backstabbing friends, and we wish we could tell them how we feel.

Courage. The ability to be confident and bold—no matter what. Today it's time to get a new level of boldness in your life. Here's how we're going to start.

Go get the cardboard center of a roll of toilet paper. If you don't have an empty roll of toilet paper, you can easily pull the cardboard tube out of any toilet paper roll you find. Once you've got the cardboard roll, write on it one thing in your life that you need courage for. You can write something specific, like the name of a person you need to confront, or you can write something more general. Next fill a sink with water and put your cardboard roll in the water. Completely submerge it until it's waterlogged and will stay under by itself.

Now watch what happens. Your cardboard will get extremely soft. It'll start to pull apart from itself. Pretty soon you won't have a cardboard tube, you'll have an odd-shaped piece of cardboard.

What's happening to the tube symbolizes what happens to you when you try to face the thing you wrote on it without courage. You live like a wet piece of cardboard. You're flimsy, pliable, and easily reshaped by something that shouldn't have power over you. You allow another thing to rule your courage and keep it tamed. But who wants to live like that warped, flimsy tube?

Today, use the courage that God gave you to deal with the thing you wrote on the tube. Act on your courage and confront in love. Act on your courage and do the thing that God is leading you to do, no matter what.

See, you can live your life like a wet piece of cardboard: limp, soaked, useless. Or you can live with boldness. You can live with courage.

Live It Strong

- What have you learned about courage from this activity?
- Using what you've learned from this illustration, how would you explain the importance of courage to your best friend?
- How can you apply what you've learned about courage from this illustration and from Scripture to your life?

WHY SHOULD I PRACTICE SPIRITUAL DISCIPLINES?

God's Word

But as for me, it is good to be near God. I have made the Sovereign LORD my refuge; I will tell of all your deeds. Psalm 73:28

Let us draw near to God with a sincere heart in full assurance of faith, having our hearts sprinkled to cleanse us from a guilty conscience and having our bodies washed with pure water. Hebrews 10:22

Submit yourselves, then, to God. Resist the devil, and he will flee from you. Come near to God and he will come near to you. Wash your hands, you sinners, and purify your hearts, you double-minded. James 4:7–8

Live It

What does it take to be close to God? Do you have to pray all the time? Are you required to fast once a week? How about tithing? Worship? Scripture memory? On the lines below, write down a few ideas you have about what it takes to get close to God.

_____

_____

_____

_____

No matter who you talk to, everyone has a different idea about what it takes to get close to God. Some people will tell you that you're guaranteed a close relationship with God if you'll devote thirty minutes a day to prayer and Bible study. Others will tell you that getting closer to God involves regular worship. Others will tell you that you've got to fast or that you should meditate on a psalm.

The truth is that God calls all of us to approach him differently. Some of us get close to God through regular, deep, honest prayer. Others of us can become more intimate with God through memorizing Scripture. Still others of us cleanse our bodies and souls through weekly fasting. A variety of disciplines can create intimacy with God and help you in your walk with him. Here's a short list of a few of them:

Why Should I Practice Spiritual Disciplines?

- *prayer*—simply talking to God regularly
- *fasting*—skipping a meal and spending that time in prayer
- *Scripture memory*—training your mind to meditate on God's Word
- *silence*—getting quiet so you can hear God's voice

Think through the list above. Which one fits you? Are you more of a pray-er? Does fasting help you in your walk with God? Is your strength Scripture memory?

This week we're taking on our spiritual disciplines and refining our walk with God. Spiritual disciplines allow us to get close to him and cause a normally disconnected, distant relationship to become intimate. This happens through effort, devotion, and passion, so that's what this week will go for.

Let's get started.

Live It Strong

- Why do you think spiritual disciplines are important?
- What makes practicing one of the disciplines listed above difficult for you?
- What can you change in your life this week to add the practice of one discipline?

God's Word

Oh, how I love your law! I meditate on it all day long. Psalm 119:97

If you call out for insight and cry aloud for understanding, and if you look for it as for silver and search for it as for hidden treasure, then you will understand the fear of the LORD and find the knowledge of God. Proverbs 2:3–5

When you fast, do not look somber as the hypocrites do, for they disfigure their faces to show men they are fasting. Matthew 6:16

Live It

My parents never disciplined me. Well, okay. *Sometimes* they disciplined me. But they didn't always discipline me because of the trick I learned when I was a little kid.

I learned this one from my friend across the street. Every day Ron and I would get together, and every day he'd tell me a new thing he'd come up with to keep his parents from spanking him. Ron was the king of getting out of punishment. When he did something wrong and his parents wanted to discipline him for it, Ron found a creative way of getting out of it. He'd act like he was sick and pretend he was throwing up. Or he'd pretend he was really, really sorry, and they wouldn't punish him. But the best one I heard from Ron was the "run and yell" method.

The run and yell pretty much went like you're thinking. If your dad came to spank you for something, you'd just run. You'd run as fast as you could. You'd run like you were being chased by Martians who had already vaporized your entire family. Running is a good way to get out of a spank, but what makes this method even better is the whole yelling part. You get up to full speed and run your way out of your house. Your dad, wanting to punish you, will no doubt want to chase you. When you've made your way outside, you begin to yell. Yelling pretty much anything works, but the best things to yell are things like, "No, Dad! Don't hurt me!" and stuff like that. My dad never would have hurt me, but that didn't matter, because he sure didn't want anyone to think he would!

Since we were younger, faster, quicker, and most importantly louder than our parents, this method worked well. Ron was right: Your parents tire easily. They embarrass even easier.

66

I've looked at discipline this way my entire life. When it's time to get punished, duck and cover. When a spanking is coming, get running. So when I first heard of spiritual disciplines, I figured it's a good time to run, what should I yell? But when I was in college I discovered that spiritual disciplines aren't about punishment, they're about closeness. Spiritual disciplines don't have anything to do with punishment or teaching us what we've done wrong. They are really about getting closer to God and deepening our relationship with him.

What are they? Spiritual disciplines are simple things you practice out of a hunger to be closer to God. They are things like . . .

- silent prayer in quiet places—praying in places where you can actually pray and concentrate on what you're saying to God
- meditating—taking time to read a passage of Scripture and think it through, maybe reading through it several times to just let God's Word soak into you
- fasting—skipping a meal and spending that time in prayer or meditating on God's Word is a great way to get closer to God and let him see your devotion

It took me years to realize that spiritual disciplines aren't about punishment. They're not about running away from my heavenly Father, they're all about running toward him. They're not about yelling, "Don't hurt me!" and they're all about crying, "Lord, help me grow!" We so often look at the opportunity to exercise spiritual disciplines and freak out, head for the backyard, yell, and try to outrun God. But disciplines are really all about running *to* God.

So do that. Today, look for moments of solitude when you can think, meditate, and pray. Fast. Read God's Word. Pray. Think. Use these disciplines to run to God.

Live It Strong

- Why is getting close to God so important?
- Can you get close to God without practicing spiritual disciplines? How?
- Which of the disciplines listed above would be the most difficult for you? Which one would be easiest?

God's Word

Immediately, something like scales fell from Saul's eyes, and he could see again. He got up and was baptized, and after taking some food, he regained his strength. Saul spent several days with the disciples in Damascus. At once he began to preach in the synagogues that Jesus is the Son of God. Acts 9:18–20

As his custom was, Paul went into the synagogue, and on three Sabbath days he reasoned with them from the Scriptures, explaining and proving that the Christ had to suffer and rise from the dead. Acts 17:2–3

For what I received I passed on to you as of first importance: that Christ died for our sins according to the Scriptures, that he was buried, that he was raised on the third day according to the Scriptures. 1 Corinthians 15:3–4

Live It

Trying to get away and study God's Word can feel like a huge job, right? You wonder if having your devotions or spending time in prayer really does you any good. Sometimes you feel like you're just pushing minutes off the table into a bottomless bucket of wasted time and endless prayers.

I know how that feels. That's how I felt until I was reading through the book of Acts and noticed Paul's actions after he met Jesus. Remember Paul's conversion? He's the guy who met Jesus on his way to persecute more Christians. His plans were changed when Jesus stopped him, spoke to him, and changed his life.

What happened after Paul met Jesus demonstrates the best actions believers can take to get to know God and grow in him. Take a few minutes to read the passages listed in the God's Word section and see how Paul got to know God better.

Notice what Paul did? As soon as his eyes were healed after his conversion, he took time to learn from the disciples. He got ready to go out and preach. He knew the Scriptures inside and out.

How did Paul grow in his knowledge of God?

Through study.

How did Paul know the heart of God? How was he able to debate God's truth with people?

Through study.

How did Paul know that all of his accomplishments in life didn't earn God's attention?

Through studying God's Word.

The study of God's Word is a unique and necessary spiritual discipline. I think studying God's Word is the most important spiritual discipline we can perfect. How else can we know God's will for us? How are we supposed to know what sin is? How can we know God's passion for us? All of that knowledge is found in God's Word. And the way we uncover that kind of stuff is through regular reading and study of God's Word.

How do you perfect the discipline of the study of God's Word?

1. You've got to actually study it. You can't just read a passage and let that be all you do. Get a Bible that has study notes in it. Borrow a Bible commentary from your pastor and read what it says about the passages you're reading.
2. You've got to make studying God's Word a habit. Some of us can't handle studying the Bible at 3:00 P.M. on Tuesday and then at 9:00 P.M. on Thursday. Some of us need to actually schedule certain times to study God's Word because if we don't schedule it, we'll never do it. Others of us are the exact opposite, and that's totally cool.

Trying to study God's Word can feel like such a chore. But have you ever checked out Paul's life? He had a huge impact on the world. It began with his deep study of God's Word. Want to have an impact on the world? Imitate Paul. Study God's Word.

Live It Strong

- How does studying God's Word affect our relationship with him?
- What is the best way for you to study God's Word?
- When is the best time for you to study God's Word? Morning? Evening? What will you study tomorrow?

God's Word

See, I have taught you decrees and laws as the LORD my God commanded me, so that you may follow them in the land you are entering to take possession of it. Observe them carefully, for this will show your wisdom and understanding to the nations, who will hear about all these decrees and say, "Surely this great nation is a wise and understanding people." Deuteronomy 4:5–6

How can a young man keep his way pure? By living according to your word. I seek you with all my heart; do not let me stray from your commands. I have hidden your word in my heart that I might not sin against you. Psalm 119:9–11

We know that we have come to know him if we obey his commands. The man who says, "I know him," but does not do what he commands is a liar, and the truth is not in him. 1 John 2:3–4

Live It

Trying to get close to God can feel like climbing a mountain of mud. You get so far up, then slide back down. You grab at roots and branches only to get stuck or fall backward. You get your footing just a bit and then lose it in the slick, nasty mud. Your feet get stuck and there's no way of moving forward.

That's what trying to get to know God can feel like—never getting as close as you want. Sometimes the desire is enough. No matter how difficult the climb is, the more you climb, the better your relationship with God gets. At other times the desire doesn't seem to be enough. The more you try, the more distant you feel from God.

When God seems completely untouchable, when living for him seems impossible, when knowing him seems more a perfected art than something everyone can do, and when we feel completely lost, how do we climb the mountain up to God? How do we get access to God?

The Bible helps us. Check out Psalm 119:9–11. The way of purity, holiness, and loving God is pointed out in these verses. Take a look at them, and then read on.

70

Living according to your word. Does your life match God's Word? What does it mean to have a life that matches God's Word? It means that the way faithful believers are described in Scripture is the way you live. The principles for following God, for loving other believers, for tithing, for everything described in the Bible as being the character of the Christian—those descriptions have to describe you, too.

I have hidden your word in my heart. How in the world do you hide God's Word in your heart? Memorizing God's Word happens differently for each of us. Some of us have to repeat the passage over and over in our minds. Others just need to read it once. Some people have an amazing ability to memorize Scripture. However you do it and however difficult it is for you, it's essential that you spend time reading God's Word and committing it to memory.

That I might not sin against you. Everyone needs a system to keep themselves from sinning. Some of us can handle getting close to a rough situation without sinning. Others of us have to keep ourselves way away from even the hint of sin. The key to not sinning is to keep God's Word in your heart and then obey it. When you're tempted to sin, recalling God's Word can prevent you from making a serious mistake.

There's no easy answer to feeling separated from God. There's no cut and dry solution for when you've tried everything and still feel like God is distant. When you've messed up and don't know how to get back in touch with God, his Word directs you back to him.

Live It Strong

- How does studying God's Word help us get close to him?
- Can you fully know God without studying his Word?
- Why is memorizing God's Word important?

71

God's Word

I am the vine; you are the branches. If a man remains in me and I in him, he will bear much fruit; apart from me you can do nothing. John 15:5

Whatever happens, conduct yourselves in a manner worthy of the gospel of Christ. Then, whether I come and see you or only hear about you in my absence, I will know that you stand firm in one spirit, contending as one man for the faith of the gospel. Philippians 1:27

Therefore, since we are surrounded by such a great cloud of witnesses, let us throw off everything that hinders and the sin that so easily entangles, and let us run with perseverance the race marked out for us. Hebrews 12:1

Live It

When I was a kid, I raced BMX bikes. Honestly, I wasn't that good. Still, I always tried my best to get ready for each race. My friends and I would ride all over town. We'd practice jumps. We'd set up mock races to push each other to do our best. Training wasn't always easy, but it was always fun.

Consider the training you go through to accomplish the things that are important to you.

- Distance runners work out and run miles before they're ready for a race.
- Swimmers do lap after lap to improve their times before they're ready for a meet.
- Debate teams go over facts, discuss strategy, and set up mock debates before their meets.
- Football teams do two-a-days, work out together, eat right, and get strategies together before they play on the field.

It's all about the conditioning, isn't it? It's all about the training and the preparation, getting yourself ready to face the opposition. Getting yourself ready to do your best. That's what training is all about. What does it take to accomplish spiritual closeness to God? What kind of heart and endurance do you need to actively pursue God?

The endurance of an athlete. The same effort it takes to get ready for a game is required for spiritual disciplines. No slacking off. No taking it easy on yourself. Endurance is pushing yourself and not giving up.

The focus of a thinker. Have you ever noticed how too much thinking gives you a headache? Prayer. Study. These things require deep thinking. It's not always easy to think deeply about spiritual issues. It takes effort. But it's worth it.

The heart of a child. Formula and rules only go so far. Along with thinking and training, simple trust and faith in Jesus—the kind a child has—is an essential element in spiritual disciplines. Be always looking for the new discovery, always amazed at the face of Jesus, and always looking to sit in his lap.

The passion of someone in love. Passion is the desire to be with someone. The desire to love them beyond worldly explanation or expectation. The passionate person works tirelessly to get to know God.

If you play a sport or are part of any kind of team, you already know about these principles. And you already know what it takes to prepare. Spiritual disciplines are the same way. It's all about preparation and getting close to God.

So you've read this far this week, and you're wondering if you have what it takes to practice spiritual disciplines. You're not sure that you have the strength to actively pursue God deeply.

Remember: Endurance. Focus. Heart. Passion. If you put the same effort into following God that you already invest in the other important things in your life, your walk with God will deepen and grow stronger.

Live It Strong

- Which describes your personal pursuit of God? Sprinter? Distance runner? Bench sitter?
- Why is passion an important element in your pursuit of God?
- What gets in the way of your getting to know God better?

73

God's Word

"Even now," declares the LORD, "return to me with all your heart, with fasting and weeping and mourning." Rend your heart and not your garments. Return to the LORD your God, for he is gracious and compassionate, slow to anger and abounding in love, and he relents from sending calamity. Joel 2:12–13

When you fast, do not look somber as the hypocrites do, for they disfigure their faces to show men they are fasting. I tell you the truth, they have received their reward in full. But when you fast, put oil on your head and wash your face, so that it will not be obvious to men that you are fasting, but only to your Father, who is unseen; and your Father, who sees what is done in secret, will reward you. Matthew 6:16–18

To some who were confident of their own righteousness and looked down on everybody else, Jesus told this parable: "Two men went up to the temple to pray, one a Pharisee and the other a tax collector. The Pharisee stood up and prayed about himself: 'God, I thank you that I am not like other men—robbers, evildoers, adulterers—or even like this tax collector. I fast twice a week and give a tenth of all I get.' But the tax collector stood at a distance. He would not even look up to heaven, but beat his breast and said, 'God, have mercy on me, a sinner.' I tell you that this man, rather than the other, went home justified before God. For everyone who exalts himself will be humbled, and he who humbles himself will be exalted." Luke 18:9–14

Live It

Bill always eats too much at lunch. That's actually what makes it so cool to eat with him. When you sit down for lunch, Bill's bag is always bigger and fuller than yours. The best thing about eating lunch with Bill is the two desserts he always brings. Bill isn't a big guy, but he eats big. And on those days when your mom packs a less than average lunch, it's helpful to eat with Bill. He always has tons of food, and he's always willing to share.

Except for today.

Why Should I Practice Spiritual Disciplines?

Bill showed up today without any lunch. And when you asked him about it, you got this long story. Seems that Bill has been reading a book about getting closer to God. One of the ideas in the book was to fast one meal each day. Bill told his parents, and they completely freaked out. His dad said that fasting was silly, and his mom gave him a long speech about how his body is still growing and he needs all the nutrition it can get.

Still, Bill thinks he wants to try fasting. He tells you that he's set a goal to fast through all his lunches for the entire week. At the end of the week he'll evaluate what he's learned. To fool his parents Bill lets his mom pack a lunch every morning, but he just gives it away to people before lunch. He promises that tomorrow he'll save his desserts for you.

You understand Bill's point—he feels that fasting will help him get closer to God. But you've also heard that fasting isn't that good for your body and can actually hurt you, especially when you're young. You talked to your parents that night and your dad said, "No. Don't you even think about fasting. You're too young. It's not good for you."

You understand your dad, and you understand Bill. But what's the *right* way to look at it?

Live It Strong

- What does the Bible say about fasting?
- Is fasting ever a bad decision? Why?
- How would you help Bill understand fasting better?

God's Word

When I consider your heavens, the work of your fingers, the moon and the stars, which you have set in place. . . . O LORD our Lord, how majestic is your name in all the earth! Psalm 8:3, 9

May the words of my mouth and the meditation of my heart be pleasing in your sight, O LORD, my Rock and my Redeemer. Psalm 19:14

When you fast, do not look somber as the hypocrites do, for they disfigure their faces to show men they are fasting. I tell you the truth, they have received their reward in full. But when you fast, put oil on your head and wash your face, so that it will not be obvious to men that you are fasting, but only to your Father, who is unseen; and your Father, who sees what is done in secret, will reward you. Matthew 6:16–18

Live It

It's not easy to get yourself trained to do spiritual disciplines. For some of us it means completely changing our lifestyles. Some of us aren't wired to easily spend hours meditating on a Bible passage or to give up a meal.

But getting close to God often involves huge changes in our routines. If getting to know God is important to us, then giving up something like our time or a meal is essential. Have you ever been so hungry that you couldn't stand it? Have you ever been so hungry that you'd chew your arm off just to get something in your stomach? That's the perfect example of spiritual disciplines: being so hungry for God that you'll do anything to get close to him. If you want God so badly, then missing a meal or spending an extended amount of time in prayer doesn't seem like anything compared to filling your heart with more of God.

So today, try one of the disciplines. You've got a few options for today. Read through the list and choose one of the following things to do today to get close to God.

1. *Fast during lunch.* Let your parents know that you're going to skip lunch, and then spend that time praying. If you're at school

you'll have to find a quiet place you can be alone to pray. Spend this time meditating on God, telling him how much you love him, and thinking about what he's like and anything else that God brings to your mind.

2. *Spend time in silence.* Today after school or for at least an hour in the evening, spend time in complete and total silence. Don't watch television, don't listen to music, just sit in total and complete silence. Think about God. What's his personality like? What do you think he looks like? Imagine that you're standing in front of him—what would you say?

3. *Meditate on Scripture.* In the morning before school or just before you go to bed, read a short passage of Scripture at least five times slowly. As you're reading, think about the meaning of each word and of the entire passage.

The most important thing about spiritual disciplines is to stretch yourself. Don't take the easy road and allow yourself to skimp here. Don't allow yourself to give in and take an easy road to getting to know God better—because there aren't any easy roads. Once you've tried each of the disciplines I've listed above, choose the one you're most comfortable with and do it at least once a week.

Spiritual disciplines aren't the easiest things to begin, but they're an awesome way to deepen your relationship with God.

Live It Strong

- What have you learned about spiritual disciplines from this activity?
- Using what you've learned from this illustration, how would you explain the importance of spiritual disciplines to your best friend?
- How can you apply what you've learned about spiritual disciplines from this illustration and from Scripture to your life?

77

WHY
SHOULD I
CARE
ABOUT
SPIRITUAL
WARFARE?

ONE

's Word

When the servant of the man of God got up and went out early the next morning, an army with horses and chariots had surrounded the city. "Oh, my lord, what shall we do?" the servant asked. "Don't be afraid," the prophet answered. "Those who are with us are more than those who are with them." And Elisha prayed, "O LORD, open his eyes so he may see." Then the LORD opened the servant's eyes, and he looked and saw the hills full of horses and chariots of fire all around Elisha. 2 Kings 6:15–17

Put on the full armor of God so that you can take your stand against the devil's schemes. For our struggle is not against flesh and blood, but against the rulers, against the authorities, against the powers of this dark world and against the spiritual forces of evil in the heavenly realms. Ephesians 6:11–12

Be self-controlled and alert. Your enemy the devil prowls around like a roaring lion looking for someone to devour. 1 Peter 5:8

Live It

Ever seen the movie *The Invisible Man*? If you haven't, here's a quick synopsis: A doctor who has been experimenting with different formulas tests his potion on himself to see how effective it is. The doctor takes in his concoction, and slowly he becomes invisible. For the doctor, this isn't necessarily a bad thing. He can change things in rooms and disrupt people, and they never know who or what is making the trouble. He exists, but the people he bothers don't know he does, and they can't tell who is being annoying. After a while the doctor realizes for a variety of reasons that being invisible isn't that cool and begins to create a new kind of potion to make himself visible again.

Wouldn't you love that? Just for a day? Wouldn't it be cool to be able to mess with people without getting caught? After a while it might get old. But at first it'd probably be a great thing.

It's weird to think about the existence of another world that we can't see. It's not a world filled with invisible men but a completely different world than we know about or understand. It's a world where

80

Why Should I Care about Spiritual Warfare?

angels and demons interact with each other and work to impact our world and even us.

Have you ever felt the effects of this world? Have you ever been impacted by the unseen spiritual world? If you have, write down three ways you've been affected by it.

1. _____
   _____
2. _____
   _____
3. _____
   _____

Were you stumped? Was it difficult to think up three different ways you've been affected by the spiritual wars that the Bible says happen around you every day? Maybe, but you *have* been impacted by the spiritual realm. It affects your world and your walk with God in more ways than you might imagine.

This week we're talking about spiritual warfare. How does it affect you? Should you be concerned about it? Yeah, spiritual warfare affects you, and you should be very concerned about it. This week we'll discover why it's important to understand and what you can do to prepare yourself to fight the very real spiritual battle that God calls you to fight.

Live It Strong

- In your own words, how would you define "spiritual warfare"?
- How would you explain using "spiritual armor" to a friend?
- What can you do this week to be more aware of the spiritual world around you?

God's Word

Jesus, full of the Holy Spirit, returned from the Jordan and was led by the Spirit in the desert, where for forty days he was tempted by the devil. He ate nothing during those days, and at the end of them he was hungry. The devil said to him, "If you are the Son of God, tell this stone to become bread." Jesus answered, "It is written: 'Man does not live on bread alone.'" Luke 4:1–4 (see Luke 4:1–13)

So, if you think you are standing firm, be careful that you don't fall! No temptation has seized you except what is common to man. And God is faithful; he will not let you be tempted beyond what you can bear. But when you are tempted, he will also provide a way out so that you can stand up under it. 1 Corinthians 10:12–13

Submit yourselves, then, to God. Resist the devil, and he will flee from you. James 4:7

Live It

We're all tempted. You're tempted. I'm tempted. Your pastor, your parents, your teachers—they're all tempted. Part of being a follower of God is being tempted. When you're tempted to do something that's counter to God's plan, that's Satan at work.

How do you deal with Satan when he's on a nonstop, pedal-to-the-metal push to invade your emotions and tempt you into sinning hugely?

Immediately after Jesus was baptized, he encountered Satan. As Satan tempted him, Jesus demonstrated how we can avoid giving in to Satan's plans. The whole encounter is recorded in Luke 4:1–13. Take a few minutes to read that passage.

Did you see Jesus' ability to deflect Satan's temptations? Did you notice how Jesus was able to use simple logic and God's Word to keep from giving in to Satan's temptations? Here's some things I see in this passage.

Jesus knew Scripture. Maybe it seems like an obvious point since Jesus was God and he wrote the Bible, but it's important for us to remember. If Jesus knew God's Word, then how can we think that we don't need to know it? Knowing God's Word is our protection. When Satan tempts us, being able to recall God's Word is our shield to protect us from Satan. Do you know God's Word?

Jesus used Scripture to deflect Satan's temptations. If you don't know God's Word, then you can't use it when you're being tempted. Makes the first point seem even more important, huh? Jesus knew God's Word and how to recall it so well that when Satan tempted him, Jesus was ready. It was almost like he had a pocket full of rocks and knew exactly the right rock to throw at exactly the right time.

Jesus didn't freak out. Standing up to Satan like Jesus did can't be easy. And after such a huge moment at his baptism, experiencing the full force of Satan's temptation must have been a letdown. Imagine being tempted right after a great spiritual experience. Wouldn't you feel like something was wrong? Jesus could have lost control, and he could have gotten emotional and started blaming what was happening on someone else. Instead he keeps his cool and is able to handle Satan with strength and clarity of mind.

Jesus stood his ground. Satan didn't tempt Jesus just once; he tempted him three times. You can understand how Jesus could be strong enough for one temptation. Maybe Jesus could stand his ground through two of Satan's temptations. But three? Jesus is courageous, smart, and level-headed. He doesn't give in when Satan tries another tactic to tempt him.

How about you? Do you give in to temptation? It's easy to listen to Satan. Will you be prepared when he tempts you? What will you say? How will you use God's Word to deflect him? We're often told that imitating Jesus is important. After reading about how he handled temptation, don't you think that we should handle temptation the same way?

Live It Strong

- What are your top three temptations? Why are they so tempting?
- How have you resisted Satan in the past? What can you learn about Jesus' actions that will help you resist Satan in the future?
- What happens when we stand our ground and resist Satan? Are we stronger? Are we tempted less?

God's Word

Be careful to do everything I have said to you. Do not invoke the names of other gods; do not let them be heard on your lips. Exodus 23:13

About that time there arose a great disturbance about the Way. A silversmith named Demetrius, who made silver shrines of Artemis, brought in no little business for the craftsmen. He called them together, along with the workmen in related trades, and said: "Men, you know we receive a good income from this business. And you see and hear how this fellow Paul has convinced and led astray large numbers of people here in Ephesus and in practically the whole province of Asia. He says that man-made gods are no gods at all. There is danger not only that our trade will lose its good name, but also that the temple of the great goddess Artemis will be discredited, and the goddess herself, who is worshiped throughout the province of Asia and the world, will be robbed of her divine majesty." When they heard this, they were furious and began shouting: "Great is Artemis of the Ephesians!" Soon the whole city was in an uproar. Acts 19:23–29

Put on the full armor of God so that you can take your stand against the devil's schemes. For our struggle is not against flesh and blood, but against the rulers, against the authorities, against the powers of this dark world and against the spiritual forces of evil in the heavenly realms. Ephesians 6:11–12

Live It

I don't know if you've read much in the Bible about spiritual warfare. God's Word actually says a lot of stuff about the spiritual realm and how to deal with it. One of the best-known passages is Ephesians 6:10–18. In his letter to the believers in the city of Ephesus, Paul helps them understand how they can stand against Satan's plans.

That passage gives great instructions on how to stand up against Satan. But the passage is even better when you know the history behind why Paul wrote what he did.

Ephesus didn't always have a group of Christians living there. In fact, for the longest time the major religion in Ephesus was the worship of the pagan goddess Artemis. The people living in Ephesus were familiar with worshiping this deity, and it was part of the culture of the city. They'd offer her special offerings. They had temples built in her honor for worshiping her. But the Artemis cult wasn't the only group worshiping other gods. Other people in Ephesus had set up altars to worship other deities. They'd even set up altars to worship whoever the emperor was at the time. And there were also Jews living there. So you can imagine that when people started to become followers of Jesus, they had a huge conflict with the Jews, the Christians, and the worshipers of the pagan gods.

In fact, there was a huge conflict in Ephesus when Paul arrived on his second missionary journey. As he was traveling through the town, people began to get healed, and some became Christians. This really irritated the people who worshiped other gods, and they began to chase Paul and his group. After a long time, a lot of confusion, a small riot, and a speech by Paul, the crowd settled down and went away. Eventually Ephesus became an important city in the spread of Christianity.

Do you see the connection between the spiritual world and the physical world? Do you get how one impacts the other?

The city of Ephesus was deeply rooted in beliefs and religions that went counter to Jesus' teachings. The worship of idols and other gods went against what God commanded in the Old Testament. That devotion to other gods and worshiping idols has a connection to the spiritual realm.

Paul knew that because he had experienced it firsthand in Ephesus, and we know he did because he later writes the believers in Ephesus the important words about spiritual warfare and spiritual armor.

Paul could have just as well written those words to us today. Okay, you might not worship Artemis, but you've no doubt got all kinds of other idol options in your life. Every day there are more and more things you can give your heart to. Those things want your attention. They want you to give up following God and follow them. That's Satan's goal in spiritual warfare: to get your eyes off God and help sink you in self pity, doubt, and fighting. Paul's words help us fight back.

Live It Strong

- What idols do you worship?
- When have you experienced spiritual warfare or a connection between the spiritual world and the physical world?
- What do you think is the most important weapon we can use to resist Satan?

God's Word

When an evil spirit comes out of a man, it goes through arid places seeking rest and does not find it. Then it says, "I will return to the house I left." When it arrives, it finds the house unoccupied, swept clean and put in order. Then it goes and takes with it seven other spirits more wicked than itself, and they go in and live there. And the final condition of that man is worse than the first. That is how it will be with this wicked generation. Matthew 12:43–45

See that you do not look down on one of these little ones. For I tell you that their angels in heaven always see the face of my Father in heaven. Matthew 18:10

But even the archangel Michael, when he was disputing with the devil about the body of Moses, did not dare to bring a slanderous accusation against him, but said, "The Lord rebuke you!" Yet these men speak abusively against whatever they do not understand; and what things they do understand by instinct, like unreasoning animals—these are the very things that destroy them. Jude 9–10

Live It

God has a way of teaching you lessons in a way that makes sure you never forget it. He has a way of showing you something about a particular subject so that you can never forget the way he taught you and the lesson you needed teaching.

When I was still a new believer, I questioned whether or not the spiritual world existed. I knew that God was real, but I was very skeptical about demons, angels, and their impact on the physical world. I doubted whether demons could possess people. I doubted that angels affected our lives in any way. I made fun of people who blamed their problems on demons or spiritual warfare. Even though I was a firm believer in the existence of God, I was also a firm believer that demons were the creation of people's wild ideas and some believers' inability to accept their own failures.

I told my girlfriend (who is now my wife) that I didn't believe in the whole spiritual world thing, and she totally disagreed with me. She said, "I'll just pray about it, and God will help us see who is right about this."

And I thought I was totally safe on this one. I figured that I was so right that her praying wouldn't really make that much of a difference. The spiritual world didn't exist, and her praying couldn't change that.

God had other plans.

The more she prayed, the more weird things began to happen. Not too long after we got married, I began to learn about spiritual warfare and the reality of the spiritual world.

As we were going about our everyday lives, we would experience weird emotions. While I was inside a grocery store and she was waiting in the car, I'd experience this weird, oppressive feeling like I was going to die right then and there. When I got to the car, my wife told me that while I was in the store she felt like she was going to die. This oppressive feeling actually stayed with us the entire time we worked in that town. When I was stressed about having to give the Sunday sermon because our pastor was out of town, the night before I preached the smoke alarm in the house would go off and wake us up. We still have weird experiences from time to time. We've met people we know have spiritual problems. We've experienced situations we were sure that the demonic world was directly influencing.

Does the spiritual world exist? Do demons have a huge impact on our world? Do they affect you? Do angels protect you?

I'll be honest—I can't give you the end-all answer to all those questions. I know what I've experienced. I know that I've seen and experienced some things that have convinced me that a whole spiritual world exists. And the Bible says clearly that it does. So I can say this: Angels and demons *are* real. Demons *are* out to hurt you. There is a battle. It is real. This hasn't changed since Paul wrote the Book of Ephesians. I'm learning that the only thing that changes is how we handle the effects of the spiritual world on our lives. What we do when we're under spiritual attack is important. When we're attacked, we should run for cover under God's protection. Will you?

Live It Strong

- Have you experienced anything to convince you that the spiritual world exists?
- What should we do when we're being engaged in spiritual warfare?
- Where is God when we're under spiritual attack?

God's Word

Then he lay down under the tree and fell asleep. All at once an angel touched him and said, "Get up and eat." He looked around, and there by his head was a cake of bread baked over hot coals, and a jar of water. He ate and drank and then lay down again. The angel of the LORD came back a second time and touched him and said, "Get up and eat, for the journey is too much for you." 1 Kings 19:5–7

Suddenly an angel of the Lord appeared and a light shone in the cell. He struck Peter on the side and woke him up. "Quick, get up!" he said, and the chains fell off Peter's wrists. Then the angel said to him, "Put on your clothes and sandals." And Peter did so. "Wrap your cloak around you and follow me," the angel told him. Acts 12:7–8

Are not all angels ministering spirits sent to serve those who will inherit salvation? Hebrews 1:14

Live It

Right next to you, without you knowing it, one guy stands with a sword in his hand. He's facing out to your left. His friend is standing with an axe, facing to your right. Above you hovers another dude. Still another is walking three feet ahead of you all, keeping a constant lookout.

Your trip to the store goes as planned. Your mom picks up the celery and milk. You get the magazine your mom said you could have. And you drive away . . . right through the guy protecting you from the oncoming traffic. Right past the one holding back the driver who isn't paying attention. You get through the light, protected from the other traffic.

At home there's more of them. I can't tell you what they wear, and I can't claim to know what kind of weapons they use, but I promise you, they're in your home. They're in your room. They're watching you while you sleep.

You don't see them, but they're there. What are they doing?

Protecting.
Listening.

Helping you resist Satan.

Fighting for your survival.

Do you believe in this spiritual world? It feels kind of silly, doesn't it, to believe in an invisible world where angels and demons fight over you? It's strange to think that these beings are at war for our souls. Spiritual warfare exists on another level than anything most of us have experienced. We can't see it, and we often don't experience it either. So talking about it much makes us feel kind of strange.

What do you do about all this? Really, what's the big deal about spiritual warfare? It might affect you, but knowing about it is kind of the end of the journey, isn't it? They're there, you know they're there . . . that's pretty much it. Right?

Knowing about spiritual warfare helps us know why we're tempted, and it helps explain some of the tougher moments in the life of a Christian. Consider these ideas:

- Knowing spiritual warfare exists means that you know how to pray for yourself. You can intelligently pray things like "God, please use your angels to protect me today."
- Knowing about spiritual warfare means that you know why really messed-up things happen to you.

They say that information is power. Sometimes just knowing that there's an explanation to something helps you understand other parts of life. Just knowing that the spiritual world exists helps make sense of our struggles and experiences.

Right now spiritual beings are fighting for your survival. They are real. Their world is real. Believing in them doesn't make you a freak. Being aware of the spiritual world and cautious about it makes you wise.

Live It Strong

- How aware are you of the spiritual world in your everyday life?
- What effect has the spiritual world had on you?
- When was the last time you were aware that you were involved in spiritual warfare? What did you do?

God's Word

And these signs will accompany those who believe: In my name they will drive out demons; they will speak in new tongues. Mark 16:17

The seventy-two returned with joy and said, "Lord, even the demons submit to us in your name." He replied, "I saw Satan fall like lightning from heaven. I have given you authority to trample on snakes and scorpions and to overcome all the power of the enemy; nothing will harm you. However, do not rejoice that the spirits submit to you, but rejoice that your names are written in heaven." Luke 10:17–20

But if I drive out demons by the finger of God, then the kingdom of God has come to you. Luke 11:20

Live It

Taylor has always looked at things a little differently than other people. He's a devoted guy—attends church every time the doors are open, hangs out with the youth pastor all the time, and always seems to be reading his Bible. Taylor especially likes the passages in the Bible where someone is being affected by a demon. So Taylor often reads passages where someone is dealing with a demon or passages where Christians are told to avoid or how to deal with spiritual warfare.

Taylor's parents are pretty much the same as Taylor. Last night you had the weirdest experience at his house. When you got there Taylor's dad opened the door and gave you a tour of the house. When the tour was over, Taylor's dad turned to you.

"Did you feel the peace?"

You didn't want to be impolite, but whatever he was asking went right over your head. "I'm sorry . . . the peace?"

"Yeah," Taylor's dad continued. "Did you feel the peace? Did you feel peaceful? Were you aware of the presence of Jesus in this house? People who visit us tell us that they feel an overwhelming sense of the presence of Jesus when they come to our home."

Why Should I Care about Spiritual Warfare?

You didn't want to disappoint him, so you just went along with it. You're a guest, and guests are supposed to be polite. "Yeah, it does seem peaceful. Why is it so calm here?"

Taylor's dad then told you the strangest story you'd ever heard. "When we first moved in, we were awakened every night by something pounding on the walls in the hallway. Every night—especially the nights when I had to help lead the church service the next morning—we'd hear something weird happening in the hallway. It got really, really bad. We told our pastor, and that's when he told us about spirits, demons, and how we ought to have this house exorcised. So one night he came over and we prayed over each room in the house. Since then we've felt this strange peace throughout the house."

Just then Taylor walked up, and his dad went to help with dinner. You thought that Taylor would think what his dad said was pretty weird, so you said, "Hey, Taylor, your dad told me about 'the hallway.' You've got strange parents."

Taylor looked a little offended by your comment. "What's so weird about them?"

Okay. You're not sure if Taylor and his dad are kidding, or if the whole family is nuts.

Live It Strong

- What questions might you ask Taylor to help you understand more about what his dad said?
- How would you use what you've learned this week about spiritual warfare in talking with Taylor?
- If Taylor's parents say their experiences were real, would you feel comfortable spending time in the house? Why or why not?

God's Word

For though we live in the world, we do not wage war as the world does. The weapons we fight with are not the weapons of the world. 2 Corinthians 10:3–4

For our struggle is not against flesh and blood, but against the rulers, against the authorities, against the powers of this dark world and against the spiritual forces of evil in the heavenly realms. Ephesians 6:12

For by him all things were created: things in heaven and on earth, visible and invisible, whether thrones or powers or rulers or authorities; all things were created by him and for him. Colossians 1:16

Live It

Defining and describing spiritual warfare isn't the easiest thing. First you've got to believe that the whole spiritual world exists. Then you've got to believe that the spiritual world can affect our world. And spiritual warfare isn't the most fun thing to talk about with people. Some think it's just creepy. Others don't believe in it. And sometimes it seems like the people who do believe in spiritual warfare are a little *too* caught up in it.

But how do you describe what's happening in your world when you know that spiritual warfare is happening? The best way to describe it or even explain it is to look at something that is tied to this world but also difficult to grasp. So try this.

On a sunny day grab a piece of chalk and stand outside. Do your best to draw your shadow. This will take some work. I suggest trying it in small segments. Stand still and see where your shadow lands, then kneel down and draw part of it. Then stand again in the same position you were standing before. Then kneel again and try to draw another part of it. Repeat this over and over until you've completely drawn your shadow.

What does this have to do with spiritual warfare?

1. It teaches you that the spiritual world constantly changes. This is a world and a realm that isn't subject to the natural laws that we live under. Things in the spiritual world change, act, and react in different ways than in the natural world.

2. It teaches you to look for obscure things. The spiritual world isn't the kind of world that you can see with your human eyes. But it's not an invisible world either—it's just not visible with our human eyes. We can't see it directly, but we can "see" what's happening around us. Like your shadow, the spiritual world resembles our world, but it's an intangible version of our world.

3. It teaches you to be aware of the weirdest things. Your shadow isn't you, but when the sun hits you just right, your shadow resembles your form. Stopping to think about your shadow is kind of weird. Who stops to ponder their shadow? What's the big deal about it anyway? Same with the spiritual world. It's a weird thing to think about, but it's still a very real world. It's something you didn't think about much but that you need to know exists.

Live It Strong

- What have you learned about spiritual warfare from this activity?
- Using what you've learned from this illustration, how would you explain spiritual warfare to your best friend?
- How can you apply what you've learned about spiritual warfare from this illustration and from Scripture to your life?

93

WHY
SHOULD I
TRUST
GOD?

God's Word

*Trust in the LORD with all your heart and lean not on your own
understanding; in all your ways acknowledge him, and he will make your
paths straight. Proverbs 3:5–6*

*The LORD is good, a refuge in times of trouble. He cares for those who trust
in him. Nahum 1:7*

*May the God of hope fill you with all joy and peace as you trust in him, so
that you may overflow with hope by the power of the Holy Spirit. Romans
15:13*

Live It

Here's a quick bunch of challenges to get your mind thinking about
trust. Do your best to complete each of these. You might want to find
a friend and attempt these together.

- draw a picture of air
- describe a sunset
- explain how they put an entire movie on one small DVD disk

Were any of those difficult? I bet they were. I bet you read at least
one of those and said to yourself "Huh?!" and skipped it. I bet you
had difficulty with one of those because it just seems too impossible
to accomplish.

Isn't that like trusting God? Doesn't trusting God seem as impossible
as drawing air? You know air exists, right? So why can't you draw it?
You know God exists, right? So, why can't you trust him completely?
Why is trusting God so difficult? Why does letting God direct your
dating relationships, your schoolwork, and your friendships seem so
difficult?

Is it because you can't see God?

Is it because you can't touch God?

Is it because sometimes God feels completely present and other times he feels impossible to understand or contact?

Do you have difficulty trusting God? For what? Take a minute to write down a few things that you have difficulty trusting God about.

_____

_____

_____

_____

This week we're refining and enhancing our understanding of what it means to trust God, and we're working on our ability to trust him more. Those things you wrote above are difficult to trust God for or about. This week we'll talk about those things, and you'll discover that trusting God is difficult—but not impossible.

Live It Strong

- Why is trusting God sometimes so difficult?
- What things in your life prevent you from trusting God?
- What can you do this week to trust God more?

God's Word

I tell you the truth, whoever hears my word and believes him who sent me has eternal life and will not be condemned; he has crossed over from death to life. John 5:24

Do not conform any longer to the pattern of this world, but be transformed by the renewing of your mind. Then you will be able to test and approve what God's will is—his good, pleasing and perfect will. Romans 12:2

I can do everything through him who gives me strength. Philippians 4:13

Live It

Putting together a book isn't the easiest thing to do. It sounds easy, but it's not. You've got to have a great idea. Then you've got to be able to communicate the idea in a way publishers and editors will like. Somewhere along the way, you've got to get a table of contents together. For me the table of contents is essential. When I'm working on a project, carrying a contents list around with me really helps. As ideas come to mind, I write them down in the right spot on the contents. It's really helpful.

Recently I had the table of contents for this book with me during a Sunday worship service. My youngest daughter wanted to write me a letter during the service. I didn't have anything else for her to write on, so I handed her the table of contents for this book and allowed her to write whatever she wanted. A few minutes later she'd written the following (in adorable five-year-old language—I've translated it and cleaned it up for you):

"I love my daddy. He is the best."

I'll admit it, I was kind of annoyed. I don't like having my notes messed with. I was glad that she wanted to write me a note, but still, it's not too fun to try to decipher your notes when they're covered with someone else's.

About one minute after being annoyed with my daughter, God spoke to me through what she had done. God showed me that my daughter's writing on my notes is a lot like my writing on God's plan for my life. Here's how.

God has a plan for us. Whatever that plan is, it remains in God's possession, and he lets us know what his plan for us is a little at a time. It's like looking at a table of contents page a little at a time. God's plan for us doesn't change, and he doesn't edit what he's planned for us to do. God gives us this plan as a gift. With his plan he offers protection, provision, and the giftedness to accomplish what he wants us to do.

Then there's us. Like my daughter writing on my planned contents page for this book, we often write our own ideas on the page. We turn God's paper over and begin writing our own plan on the back. We rewrite his plan. We add our own stuff, our own dreams, our own goals, and even our own will. And we keep writing, still on God's paper, never turning the paper over to see what God has written. For some reason we like our own writing, and we love making our own plan.

God's table of contents for you is so unbelievably awesome. What he's written on the page of your life is something so cool it makes your plan look stupid. We've got to trust him and let him reveal his plan to us one section at a time. And we've got to let him hold the paper. We have to trust God's writing. We have to trust God's plan.

So put down your pencil and give God back his paper. He's waiting to show you his next chapter in your life.

Live It Strong

- When have you tried to rewrite God's plan for your life?
- Why is it difficult to obey God's plans for us?
- What do you think is on God's table of contents for your life?

God's Word

When I am afraid, I will trust in you. In God, whose word I praise, in God I trust; I will not be afraid. What can mortal man do to me? Psalm 56:3–4

Trust in the LORD with all your heart and lean not on your own understanding; in all your ways acknowledge him, and he will make your paths straight. Proverbs 3:5–6

Surely God is my salvation; I will trust and not be afraid. The LORD, the LORD, is my strength and my song; he has become my salvation. Isaiah 12:2

Live It

Ever done a trust fall? To do a trust fall you get a group of people together, and the group stands behind you while you stand with your back to them on something tall like a table or a car. When the group is ready, you fall backward onto them, and they catch you. It's like a controlled stage dive. Trust falls aren't the easiest thing for some people to do. You've got to have coordination (so you don't freak out and throw your hands all over the place), and you've got to believe in the people you're falling onto. You've got to trust the group below you enough to have confidence that they'll catch you when you fall onto them.

Trust falls teach you a variety of things. When you do one you're learning that you can trust your friends, and you're growing together as a group. When your friends catch you, you learn that you can depend on them, and they learn that they're there to hold you up and help you out. After experiencing a few trust falls together, you and your friends realize that you really can trust each other and rely on each other. Your hands and arms really are strong enough to hold each other up.

What if you had just a two-man trust fall? Let's say it was just you and your best friend. You're on the back of a truck and your friend is standing below. Your friend's arm is outstretched, palms up. And you're standing with your back to your friend, eyes closed, ready to fall.

100

Would you? Do you trust your friend enough to catch you? Do you believe in your friend's strength enough to fall backward?

Maybe not, because one person isn't that strong. But what if that friend was God and you were standing in the exact same place. What if God were on the ground yelling, "Do it! Fall backward! Don't you trust me?" Could you do it?

Trusting God sounds like the simplest thing in the world. Knowing God's power and what he's done in the past, we can easily sit where we are and say that we trust him enough to fall backward. But when we're in a place where we actually have to trust God, our reaction can be entirely different. For example, consider this list. Can you:

- trust God to help you during final exams
- trust God for the right college to go to
- trust God for a successful future after high school and college
- trust God for the right date for the dance

No, those aren't literal falls backward, but think about it. Every time you look out at the horizon of your life, you see something you have to trust God for. What's ahead—your classes, college, marriage—are all things that involve you trusting God. And it's exactly like a trust fall. You are closing your eyes and falling backward into God's huge, powerful hands.

Ever stopped to think about God's hands? His hands created the universe. His hands disciplined the Israelites. His hands were nailed to the cross. His hands formed you. Can't you imagine that hands like his, hands that have done so much, are totally capable and powerful enough to direct and care for your future?

Live It Strong

- What issue are you struggling with trusting God about right now?
- Why is it easier to make our own plans rather than trust God's plan for us?
- What are the benefits of trusting God?

God's Word

While he was saying this, a ruler came and knelt before him and said, "My daughter has just died. But come and put your hand on her, and she will live." Matthew 9:18

A large crowd followed and pressed around him. And a woman was there who had been subject to bleeding for twelve years. . . . When she heard about Jesus, she came up behind him in the crowd and touched his cloak, because she thought, "If I just touch his clothes, I will be healed." Immediately her bleeding stopped and she felt in her body that she was freed from her suffering. Mark 5:25, 27–29

"'If you can'?" said Jesus. "Everything is possible for him who believes." Immediately the boy's father exclaimed, "I do believe; help me overcome my unbelief!" Mark 9:23–24

Live It

Approaching Jesus must have been intimidating. As his ministry grew and his teachings became more well known, each town he entered became either a city-wide pep rally or a riot, depending on the people's reaction. The more it was like a riot, the bigger the crowds. The bigger the crowds, the more difficult it was to get to Jesus. It must have been difficult for the lame to get close to get healed. It had to be almost impossible for Jesus to touch every beggar. Imagine Jesus desiring to heal people but not being able to get to each hurting person. Imagine him passionately wanting to reach the broken but facing too many broken people.

That's what makes the story of the woman who was healed one day so cool. Read it in Mark 5:25–34. This woman had been bleeding from some part of her body for years. Others knew about her bleeding problem, it grossed them out, and the woman was basically ignored and disliked by the entire community. So this woman went after Jesus—not because she wanted clarification on the laws about blood, and not so she could get close to Jesus so that the world would see that he accepted her. Nah. This woman's problem was so bad that she only wanted one thing. She was desperate. She was looking for nothing short of healing.

You get the idea that this woman is desperate from the way the story is told in the Gospel of Mark. Mark doesn't give much detail about the woman or what she said. This woman's desperation was her connection to God. Jesus doesn't even stop to heal her, because he's actually on his way to another healing. This woman was healed because of God's power and her trust. God doesn't need our help, but something about this woman's trust makes a significant connection with Jesus. She's willing to face humiliation and to step out of her comfort zone and simply trust Jesus.

Do you see that? Simple trust.

I don't know about you, but sometimes those words sound like an unending series of "blah, blah, blah's" from your sister sitting next to you on a four-hour car ride. Really. Simply trusting Jesus. It's so easy to say and it's said so often that it can get annoying to hear it over and over.

But look at the benefits of actually trusting Jesus. This woman, with nothing to gain or lose, was healed through touch. That screams two things: (1) Jesus' power, and (2) the power of our trust in God.

We serve a *trustworthy* God. He's not only worthy of our trust because he's the Creator and Savior, he's worthy of it because with a simple touch we can be healed, too. Jesus does something with our trust that's hard to completely understand. When we place our trust in him, he reaches out to touch us.

So you're not bleeding. Okay then. What *are* you facing? What's your issue? School? Your dating relationship? Your parents?

I don't know how Jesus does it. I can't claim supernatural knowledge of how God heals or guides. I don't understand what happens when we trust God, and I don't know exactly what he does in us once we trust him. But I know that in this story, the woman only had to touch Jesus. So I say, reach out your hand. I think that when we begin to trust God, good things happen. Not necessarily right away. And not always easy things. But good things. Really, really good things.

So go ahead. Reach out and touch Jesus. Give him the thing you're struggling with. Trust him to help you and to heal you.

Live It Strong

- What thing are you struggling with that you need to give to Jesus?
- What prevents us from being honest with God and giving him our struggles?
- How does God feel when we place our entire trust in him?

God's Word

But he said to me, "My grace is sufficient for you, for my power is made perfect in weakness." Therefore I will boast all the more gladly about my weaknesses, so that Christ's power may rest on me. That is why, for Christ's sake, I delight in weaknesses, in insults, in hardships, in persecutions, in difficulties. For when I am weak, then I am strong. 2 Corinthians 12:9–10

Continue in your faith, established and firm, not moved from the hope held out in the gospel. Colossians 1:23

Here I am! I stand at the door and knock. If anyone hears my voice and opens the door, I will come in and eat with him, and he with me. Revelation 3:20

Live It

I know some students who are experiencing the fear of their future and the uncertainty of their trust in God probably the same way you might be right now.

People often think that pastors and teachers have everything together. They often look to these people as emotional rocks and spiritual guides. Especially students. I've worked with students enough to recognize that younger people often have loads of questions about their future.

When I work with college students, I get pelted with all kinds of questions and prayer requests—mostly around March and mostly about the future. March is close enough to graduation ceremonies and the end of the school year that students start to get nervous about their next step.

I'd never say that I'm an expert on your generation. I wouldn't claim to know more about you than you know about yourself. And I'd never say that I know what it's like to be a teenager today or how difficult it is to trust God at your age. Yeah, I've been there. But the world has changed since I was a student.

But based on the stories that I've heard from students I work with, I know that when you look out at the world at your age, things can sometimes look really, really scary. At your age you've got your entire life ahead of you. Huge decisions are waiting for you: College. Career. Marriage. Apartments and houses.

It's safe to say that if I were your age, I'd be freaking out. What advice could I possibly offer you?

I could say, "Trust God for your future," and then leave you with that. I mean, that's pastoral, right? That's also good advice and good, helpful counseling, right?

Yeah, it is, but just saying "trust God for your future" doesn't quite do it, does it? So here's another option that I think works better: a road map. How do you get to the place where you can trust God for those big things? Take it one turn at a time.

Try something small. For example, trust God to help you focus for an exam. Trust God to help you get along with your parents. Then when you've learned to trust God for small things, you'll understand how to trust him for those bigger, scarier things.

Live It Strong

- Is it more difficult to trust God when you're a teenager or when you're an adult? Why?
- Why does God want us to trust him?
- What small thing can you give over to God as a way to start trusting him for bigger things?

God's Word

Those who know your name will trust in you, for you, LORD, have never forsaken those who seek you. Psalm 9:10

You will keep in perfect peace him whose mind is steadfast, because he trusts in you. Trust in the LORD forever, for the LORD, the LORD, is the Rock eternal. Isaiah 26:3–4

Come to me, all you who are weary and burdened, and I will give you rest. Take my yoke upon you and learn from me, for I am gentle and humble in heart, and you will find rest for your souls. Matthew 11:28–29

Live It

You've never been comfortable thinking of yourself as a senior, but that's what you are. A senior. You're the person all the freshmen wish they could be like—with most of your high school days behind you and your entire life ahead. You've survived years of school food, endless pep rallies, proms, and even years of band camp.

You are a senior. College is just ahead of you.

And college is freaking you out. It's the endless financial aid forms. It's the scholarship contests. It's the applications.

But more than anything, it's trusting God for next year.

Your whole life you've been supported and cared for. Your secure home has been the launching pad for all kinds of adventures. But college is different. It's the adventure that begins the rest of your life. So you've applied everywhere. You've tried out for all kinds of scholarships and financial aid.

How do you feel? Scared. No other word sums up the mix of anticipation, dread, despair, joy, and uncertainty. Feeling scared isn't fun. Feeling scared while your parents are pressuring you to make decisions isn't any better.

And your friends are no help either. Phil got into the first place he applied and got a full scholarship, too. Jessica isn't going to college this year. She's taking a year to work at a city newspaper first to get some experience. Brent is going to community college his first two years to get his required classes out of the way. He got accepted immediately, and his grandparents are paying the inexpensive tuition.

Your pastor doesn't give you any good advice either. He seems to talk forever, but his advice isn't anything you haven't already heard. He says, "You've just got to trust God. It's that simple."

You've heard the whole "trust God" thing since you started searching for a college and a career, and you're just flat sick of the speech. Just trusting God doesn't feel tangible. It doesn't feel like real action. "But isn't there something I should be *doing*?" you respond to your pastor in an annoyed tone.

He fires back with, "You've already done everything you can do. You've applied. You've prepared your whole life. Let God work in you."

No. This isn't enough. At the risk of sounding unspiritual and against God's will, this kind of quick and easy answer doesn't work for you.

What do I do next? you think to yourself. With your friends easily getting their lives in order and your pastor not giving you any help, you feel alone and abandoned. You've got your whole life ahead of you but you feel like you have to travel this unknown road all alone.

Now what?

Live It Strong

- What would you do next to help you deal with the decisions you feel like you have to make?
- What makes trusting God for your future so difficult?
- How might you help your pastor understand your frustration?

God's Word

I have been crucified with Christ and I no longer live, but Christ lives in me. The life I live in the body, I live by faith in the Son of God, who loved me and gave himself for me. Galatians 2:20

So do not be ashamed to testify about our Lord, or ashamed of me his prisoner. But join with me in suffering for the gospel, by the power of God, who has saved us and called us to a holy life—not because of anything we have done but because of his own purpose and grace. 2 Timothy 1:8–9

This is the confidence we have in approaching God: that if we ask anything according to his will, he hears us. 1 John 5:14

Live It

Trusting God can be difficult. We all have problems believing that God can do what he says. Even when God has proven himself, we still have difficulty trusting him. Yeah, we know that God's Word promises that he's trustworthy. Yeah, God has proven himself to us over and over again, and we know he's worthy of our trust. But even with that information in our heads, it's still difficult to trust him.

How do you learn to trust God for everything in your life? How do you learn to trust him when he can feel so distant? How do you learn to trust him when the things in your life are so huge that no one seems strong enough to handle them?

Here's an idea. Try this.

Go get a piece of paper and a pencil. Then think about the things in your life that you have difficulty trusting God with. It's okay to put both big and small things on your list. Consider putting things like "keeping up my GPA," "getting into the right college," or even "making first string on the team." When you've written several things on the paper, spend time asking God to help you trust him for the things on the list. After you've prayed, find a place that's safe for you to burn things and burn the list you wrote. As your list is burning, say out loud, "God, I am trusting you for the things on this list. I give these things to you."

Why is burning this list important? Fire often symbolizes both a total giving something up to God and the complete destruction of things that are important. Burning your list demonstrates that you are giving them over to God so he can help you learn to trust him.

After you've burned your list, live like God is handling everything. Don't freak out about the things you put on your list. God has them under his control, and he'll accomplish the things you put on your list in the order he sees fit and in the way he chooses.

Yeah, trusting God for anything is difficult. But if you can commit a few things to God now, trusting him for the bigger stuff later will be easier.

Live It Strong

- What have you learned about trusting God?
- Using what you've learned from this illustration, how would you explain the effects of trusting God to your best friend?
- How can you apply what you've learned about trusting God from this illustration and from Scripture to your life?

WHY SHOULD I GIVE MY LIFE TO GOD?

God's Word

Then I heard the voice of the Lord saying, "Whom shall I send? And who will go for us?" And I said, "Here am I. Send me!" Isaiah 6:8

Then he said to his disciples, "The harvest is plentiful but the workers are few. Ask the Lord of the harvest, therefore, to send out workers into his harvest field." Matthew 9:37–38

"My food," said Jesus, "is to do the will of him who sent me and to finish his work. Do you not say, 'Four months more and then the harvest'? I tell you, open your eyes and look at the fields! They are ripe for harvest." John 4:34–35

Live It

I've always seen life as one big competition. Not a competition to be better than the other person, and not a competition of skill or wit. A competition for your focus.

Take a mental walk through your life. What things compete for your attention? What things compete for your focus?

- Media—television and radio scream all kinds of messages at you every day.
- Friends—well-meaning people can hinder you from completely giving your attention to God.
- Passion—believe it or not, not knowing what you're called to do can keep you from focusing on God and giving him your entire life.

112

Why should you give your life to God? You can answer that with a variety of correct answers. You should give your life to God because he asks for it. You should give your life to him because he created you. He deserves everything from you, including your entire life, because he gave his life for you.

Why Should I Give
My Life to God?

But maybe you already understand that God deserves your entire life. Maybe a better question is, *How should I give my life to God?* Do you take a picture of yourself and mail it to him? Do you pile all your stuff in the middle of your room and tell God to take it? Let's say that God visited you in a dream and told you that he wanted you to give him your entire life. How would you do that? On the lines below, write out how you might give God your entire life.

_____

_____

_____

_____

Got a grip on it? Understand how to give God your entire life?

It's not easy. And, honestly, you can give yourself and your life to anything these days. This week we'll talk about why you should give God your life and how you can turn it over to him. You can't actually physically walk up to God and give him your life. But you can offer it to him daily. You can live so boldly for him that he takes over.

Should you give God all of your life? How? That's what we'll tackle this week.

Live It Strong

- Why is it important to give your life to God?
- What things in your life prevent you from giving your life to God?
- What can you do this week to completely give yourself to God?

God's Word

He who trusts in himself is a fool, but he who walks in wisdom is kept safe.
Proverbs 28:26

Now a man named Ananias, together with his wife Sapphira, also sold a piece of property. With his wife's full knowledge he kept back part of the money for himself, but brought the rest and put it at the apostles' feet. Then Peter said, "Ananias, how is it that Satan has so filled your heart that you have lied to the Holy Spirit and have kept for yourself some of the money you received for the land? Didn't it belong to you before it was sold? And after it was sold, wasn't the money at your disposal? What made you think of doing such a thing? You have not lied to men but to God." When Ananias heard this, he fell down and died. Acts 5:1–5

If anyone thinks he is something when he is nothing, he deceives himself.
Galatians 6:3

Live It

When you give something to God, you'd better really give it. When you claim to have given something to God, you'd better either really have given it or be prepared to suffer the consequences of your lie.

After Jesus ascended into heaven, the apostles began to set up groups of believers who gathered together for worship and fellowship. The first few chapters of the Book of Acts record the incredible formation of the early church. God's people got together and learned what it meant to be God's people living in community. Acts tells us how they preached the gospel, how they received the Holy Spirit, how they lived, and how they loved each other. If you ever want a lesson in how Christians first lived together, read the first seven chapters of Acts.

Those first chapters also teach us about honoring God, being honest with him, and giving him what he deserves. That lesson is taught through the lives of Ananias and Sapphira (see Acts 5:1–11). The story goes that in the early days of the church, believers often sold their possessions and gave all or part of the proceeds to the church to give out to the poor and needy. Ananias and Sapphira were wealthy land-

owners who decided to sell their land and give the entire sale price to the church. Their decision wasn't that solid, and they ultimately kept part of the money for themselves.

When Peter called them to meet with him, he planned to ask a simple question. Peter wanted to know if they'd given all of the money to the church or kept some of it for themselves. Ananias told Peter that he'd given all of the money to the church. Peter knew Ananias was lying, and Ananias dropped dead right there. Peter called Sapphira and asked her pretty much the same question. When Sapphira lied, she dropped dead and was carried out to be buried.

Does God hate people who have wealth? Maybe God can't stand it when we don't give everything we have to the church? Maybe God just can't stand liars? Some of that might be true, but we learn one important thing from Ananias and Sapphira: You can't tell God that you're giving him everything and then hold back. You can't tell people that you're giving everything and then not give it.

Do you ever make promises to God and then not keep them? Hypocrisy was probably the root of Ananias and Sapphira's problem. Have you ever said you did something for God when you really didn't? Ever acted like you had your life with God together when you really didn't? Ever tried to lie to God about the things you're willing to do for him?

When I think about Ananias and Sapphira, I'm reminded of all the things I've told God I'd do for him and then skipped out on. I remember all the things I've told my friends I did for God that I've really only half done. I remember the results of Ananias and Sapphira's half truths—and I wonder about the results my hypocrisy has had on my life.

When you give your life to God, you should give it all. When you say you're going to give yourself to God, you'd better do it. Not because of the punishment that comes with half truths or hypocrisy, but because giving everything to him is really the only way to live.

Live It Strong

- Why is it important to be honest with God?
- How much damage does hypocrisy do to our relationship with God?
- What happens when we lie to God?

God's Word

The greatest among you will be your servant. Matthew 23:11

Command those who are rich in this present world not to be arrogant nor to put their hope in wealth, which is so uncertain, but to put their hope in God, who richly provides us with everything for our enjoyment. 1 Timothy 6:17

But you, dear friends, build yourselves up in your most holy faith and pray in the Holy Spirit. Keep yourselves in God's love as you wait for the mercy of our Lord Jesus Christ to bring you to eternal life. Jude 20–21

Live It

I've known a lot of pastors. My pastors have shepherded me, taught me, corrected me, and loved me throughout my life, maybe like a pastor has done for you. I've also known a lot of really great pastors' wives. They're people who live amazing lives in the shadow of their husbands. When you hear the words "pastor's wife," you may think of a kindly, godly woman who can stretch a dollar and never has anything sour to say about anyone. Pastors' wives always seem to be some of the best examples of how a spiritual woman should live.

My wife's grandmother is, in my opinion, an incredible pastor's wife. Grandma Jones is an amazingly simple woman who embodies a life completely turned over to Jesus. I think the best way to explain her to you is to lay out how wonderfully different she and her husband are from the rest of the world.

- Simple life: I've never met anyone who lives more simply. They're wonderfully content with an old way of doing things. They're not in a hurry to adopt the newest, latest, easiest, or cushiest things.
- Poverty: During their entire ministry career, their family income was right at poverty level.

- Housing: They got indoor plumbing long after their entire neighborhood got it. They were completely content with not keeping up with the changes that were taking place in other homes.
- Furniture: They've always had the "pastor's" kind of furniture, old and worn beyond that "homey" feeling.
- Trash picking: Sounds gross, but to make the financial ends meet, Grandpa Jones would sometimes pick up other people's old trash or junk, take it home, and use it. Some favorite family stories include him picking up old combs in parking lots and attempting to smuggle them into the home without Grandma Jones finding out.

It's true, being a pastor doesn't mean money or fame. Some pastors' wives don't seem to handle their husband's calling with the grace and poise required. Grandma Jones, however, stands as an awesome example of a life sold out for God. Poverty doesn't stop her. Worn furniture is no big deal. The sometimes confusing way the world is always changing, not a problem.

I'm amazed that in a world where following God can be so difficult, Grandma Jones finds a way to live above the struggle for surrender. It's as if her spiritual gift is the gift of surrender and being an example, like her calling is to simply demonstrate what a life given to God looks like. I wish you could meet this woman. She is the best example I can think up of how to live a life totally given to God.

What happens when you give your life to God? Among other things, you end up being an example. You're the bonfire in the winter. The smell of good food drifting through a room. You have the ability to affect others in ways you could never imagine. You have the ability to live above the mess and crud of lives without hope.

How could you *not* give yourself to God?

Live It Strong

- Are poverty and giving yourself to God connected? How?
- When you live completely for God, who might you influence?
- What makes giving your life to God difficult?

God's Word

"For I know the plans I have for you," declares the LORD, "plans to prosper you and not to harm you, plans to give you hope and a future."
Jeremiah 29:11

Many, O LORD my God, are the wonders you have done. The things you planned for us no one can recount to you; were I to speak and tell of them, they would be too many to declare. Psalm 40:5

You discern my going out and my lying down; you are familiar with all my ways. Psalm 139:3

Live It

When God sleeps and when he's awake, God has dreams for you. Is it right to imagine God sleeping? Okay, so maybe God doesn't sleep. But can you imagine God daydreaming? After a hard day of meeting needs, dealing with human frailties, and working out various problems in the world, God takes a moment to just let his mind wander. Imagine that as his mind is wandering, you pop into his head. He remembers how he formed your fingers in your mom's belly. He remembers your first steps. He remembers every hurt you've dealt with. He remembers all your joys.

And then imagine that God dreams about your future. He thinks about your abilities and passions. I imagine that God thinks about the things you can do with your passion. He imagines the things you can accomplish and the things he can call you to do.

So what do you dream of doing for God? Lets say that you had an hour to daydream and let your mind run wild. What things could you imagine that you could accomplish for God? What beyond belief dreams do you have about your life? Take a few moments to make a list of the things you'd like to accomplish for God. Don't hold back. Dream big.

_____

_____

_____

_____

Look over your list. Do you think that God dreams the same things for you? Can you imagine that God's dreams and goals for you are very similar to yours?

When I first started thinking about what I was going to do with my life, I thought that God had this rigid plan for me. I figured that before I was born, God had carved in some heavenly stone somewhere the plan that I would follow my entire life. I figured that God had designed the time I would give my life to him and then all the big and small impacts that I would make on the world. Every career move would be designed by him. Every life decision guided and controlled by the iron hand of God.

The older I get, the more I see it differently. I see God dreaming for us, kind of like a parent at a piano recital. As he sits and watches us live our lives, his head fills with the things that we could accomplish. I see God staring at us, longing for us to do great things for him. I see him dreaming about our future.

I think that as *we're* dreaming about the things we're going to do in our lives, *God* is dreaming too. And I think that as *God* is dreaming about the things we'll do in our lives, *we're* dreaming too. That's why it's important to give our entire lives to God. Imagine your life not given to God: all your dreams going unaccomplished, all God's dreams for you never happening, never living up to your potential, never accomplishing anything for God.

Why should you give your life to God? Because it's in giving your life to God that all your potential is lived out. In giving your life to God, you begin to live the destiny only God could dream up. Giving your life to God means that everything you were created to do is accomplished, and God gets the glory.

Live It Strong

- Is it realistic to think that God has dreams for you?
- Why is it important to pay attention to God's dreams for you?
- How does giving your life to God help you live his plans for you?

Week Seven

God's Word

I urge you, brothers, to watch out for those who cause divisions and put obstacles in your way that are contrary to the teaching you have learned. Keep away from them. For such people are not serving our Lord Christ, but their own appetites. By smooth talk and flattery they deceive the minds of naive people. Romans 16:17–18

For there are many rebellious people, mere talkers and deceivers, especially those of the circumcision group. They must be silenced, because they are ruining whole households by teaching things they ought not to teach—and that for the sake of dishonest gain. Even one of their own prophets has said, "Cretans are always liars, evil brutes, lazy gluttons." Titus 1:10–12

Be merciful to those who doubt; snatch others from the fire and save them; to others show mercy, mixed with fear—hating even the clothing stained by corrupted flesh. Jude 22–23

Live It

Some people are wonderful fantastic people who always seem to be at their best in awful circumstances. They never overreact. They always approach tough situations with grace. Nothing seems to rattle them.

That's the way I envision Titus. He's the pastor in the New Testament who was sent to the island of Crete. You might not know much about the island of Crete, but you might know people like the people who lived there. They were notoriously bad people. They were known as liars and backbiters, the kind of people you couldn't trust. Their reputation for nastiness preceded them. So when Titus went to Crete to tell them about Jesus, you know that he had his work cut out for him. It was the ultimate clash of worlds—the godly man confronting the pagans. Guess who won.

Paul actually began the spread of Christianity in Crete and left Titus there to organize the church. Later Paul wrote to Titus and offered instruction on the basics of organizing the church and instructing the believers. Paul's letter to the young pastor, now the Book of Titus, is typical of the kind of letter one leader would write to another.

But the interesting thing is what we know Titus' character must have been like. The man Paul chose to shape up the believers and evangelize the island of Crete must have been a rock of a guy. Paul wouldn't have left someone who was wishy-washy or who couldn't take the heat of being in the midst of nasty, backbiting sinners like the Cretans. We don't know the details of the impact Titus had on the island, but we know he did have some success. We know that Paul's initial work and Titus's continued work on Crete began a strong church there. Even though Titus faced awful people, he was able to pastor and build the church.

I don't know about you, but I don't do well around difficult people. I'm not a fan of people who enjoy being mean. I don't like backbiters or hard-to-get-along-with kinds of people. That's why I'm impressed with what Titus did. He wasn't afraid of mean people. He wasn't scared to face nasty people.

Giving your life to God can mean all kinds of things. It could mean traveling to the Congo and it could mean working in the inner city. Whatever God calls you to do, giving your life to him means that he'll place you in the perfect place to do his perfect will. Along the way you may face some tough things, like rotten people and nasty situations.

Can you give your life to God? Sure. But can you *keep* giving your life to God? Can you make it an unending stream of giving where you constantly follow God and live for him despite the nasty people God leads you to help? Can you give your life to God even though many people along the way may want to shove you off that path?

Live It Strong

- How does giving our lives to God help us deal with uncomfortable people?
- How does a life given to God help unsaved or just mean people understand God?
- Why is it important to give our lives to God?

121

God's Word

Amos answered Amaziah, "I was neither a prophet nor a prophet's son, but I was a shepherd, and I also took care of sycamore-fig trees. But the LORD took me from tending the flock and said to me, 'Go, prophesy to my people Israel.'" Amos 7:14–15

As Jesus walked beside the Sea of Galilee, he saw Simon and his brother Andrew casting a net into the lake, for they were fishermen. "Come, follow me," Jesus said, "and I will make you fishers of men." Mark 1:16–17

Every high priest is selected from among men and is appointed to represent them in matters related to God, to offer gifts and sacrifices for sins. . . . No one takes this honor upon himself; he must be called by God, just as Aaron was. Hebrews 5:1, 4

Live It

Evan always had things his own way. He's the only child from a pretty wealthy family. His parents bought him everything he wanted, and he usually bragged about what he had. He was the first kid in your school to get a brand new car after getting his driver's license. Evan had never had to work for anything in his life. Along with having rich parents, Evan was always super smart. Studying didn't just come easy for him, Evan *never* had to study. You've never met anyone as smart as Evan.

If you weren't Evan's best friend, you never would have known that he wasn't happy. If you didn't hang with Evan, you'd think that he was perfectly wired and perfectly formed. But since you were his best friend, you knew that Evan often acted like a selfish jerk. When you ate out with him, he was mean to the people working at the counter. When you went to church with him, he talked bad about the youth leaders. He'd make fun of, pick on, and act better than just about everyone he came into contact with.

You'll never forget the day Evan changed.

One Sunday Evan left right in the middle of church. In the middle of the message about serving in overseas missions, he just got up and walked out. After the service you found him sitting on the front steps of the church. He was acting too cool and too strong to cry, but you could tell what was happening.

"Dude, what's up?"

"How could you just sit there and listen?" Evan asked. His tone was snide as usual.

"What? Sit there?"

"Yeah. Doesn't it bother you what's happening over there? Didn't it bother you to hear about the kids who live with sewage running through their homes? Doesn't it bug you that those kids eat one meal each day? Don't you have a heart? How could you listen to that?"

This is weird. Usually Evan's the one without a heart. If those people lived in your town, Evan would be the first to make fun of them. "Well, I guess I didn't think about it. I guess I wasn't paying that much attention."

"Not paying attention? I need to go. I need to help those people. I can't stay here, and I can't waste my life in college. I need to go over and help."

Evan sounded serious. You'd never heard this much determination from him. You were fairly sure that with his parents' money and his brains, Evan could go if he wanted to.

Evan, the smart, rich, overconfident guy who never met someone he couldn't make fun of, had to deal with God's call to be poor and work with the people Evan had thought were unintelligent. Three weeks later, Evan told you that he'd applied to go with a mission group after graduation. Six months later, Evan put his college plans on hold and boarded a plane to Central Asia to help people living in poverty.

You meet up with Evan two years later. The man you knew doesn't exist any longer. His snide attitude has been replaced with a comfortable compassion. His "smarter than thou" attitude is now overshadowed by his willingness to help and his obvious desire to reach lives.

What does it mean to give your life to God?

Ask Evan.

Live It Strong

- Why does God often ask us to change our plans to fit his?
- What would you do to help Evan take action when he felt called?
- What Scriptures would you show Evan to help him grasp what God was calling him to do?

God's Word

Therefore, I urge you, brothers, in view of God's mercy, to offer your bodies as living sacrifices, holy and pleasing to God—this is your spiritual act of worship. Do not conform any longer to the pattern of this world, but be transformed by the renewing of your mind. Then you will be able to test and approve what God's will is—his good, pleasing and perfect will. Romans 12:1–2

Not that I have already obtained all this, or have already been made perfect, but I press on to take hold of that for which Christ Jesus took hold of me. Brothers, I do not consider myself yet to have taken hold of it. But one thing I do: Forgetting what is behind and straining toward what is ahead, I press on toward the goal to win the prize for which God has called me heavenward in Christ Jesus. Philippians 3:12–14

Therefore, since we are surrounded by such a great cloud of witnesses, let us throw off everything that hinders and the sin that so easily entangles, and let us run with perseverance the race marked out for us. Hebrews 12:1

Live It

Giving your life to God is like eating cake, right? It's like a vacation, isn't it? All you have to do is drop to your knees, say a little prayer, and then just live your life. The only thing that could be difficult is making sure you pray every day and don't sin real big. Giving your life to God is super, super easy. Right?

Wrong!

Giving your life to God involves a combination of very difficult things: submission and surrender, with serious attempts at living a holy and righteous life. Giving your life to God is exactly what "giving" sounds like—walking up to God with your past, present, and future on a silver platter, laying it at his feet, and then walking away. It's being willing to trust him to take care of your future. It's allowing him to take care of you.

Along the way you'll encounter various roadblocks. Many of these roadblocks will be things that you create and develop yourself. Loads of things keep you from completely giving your life to God, and many of those things are stuff that you create. Yeah, that's right. In the process of giving yourself to God, you are your own worst enemy.

Let's take a minute and break apart the humanly created roadblocks. Think about it: What prevents you from giving your entire self—your loves and hates, your joys, your gifts—to God? List your biggest obstacles below.

_____

_____

_____

_____

_____

If you're like me, that's one whopper of a list. The things you've written there can take loads of willpower and stamina to give up. There's no easy, magical formula for surrendering these things to God, but you can start. Here's how.

Rewrite your list on a single sheet of paper. Find a place in your room where you rarely go, like a corner, and set a chair facing out into the room. Take your list, kneel in front of the chair, and ask God out loud to help you hurdle the roadblocks you've written on the paper. Don't just kneel and pray without really seeking God. Imagine that when you're praying, you're bowing at God's feet and surrendering yourself to him completely. Picture it in your mind. Then read each roadblock you've written. Each day this week, make this part of your prayer time.

This isn't a formula for roadblock-surrendering success. But the more you do it, the more the difficulty of surrendering to God will fade and the more God will take over.

Live It Strong

- What have you learned about giving yourself to God from this activity?
- Using what you've learned from this activity, how would you explain giving yourself to God to your best friend?
- How can you apply what you've learned about giving yourself to God from this illustration and from Scripture to your life?

125

WHY SHOULD I DEFEND MY FAITH?

God's Word

Whether I am in chains or defending and confirming the gospel, all of you share in God's grace with me. Philippians 1:7

The latter do so in love, knowing that I am put here for the defense of the gospel. Philippians 1:16

Dear friends, although I was very eager to write to you about the salvation we share, I felt I had to write and urge you to contend for the faith that was once for all entrusted to the saints. For certain men whose condemnation was written about long ago have secretly slipped in among you. They are godless men, who change the grace of our God into a license for immorality and deny Jesus Christ our only Sovereign and Lord. Jude 1:3–4

Live It

Imagine you were given a diamond the size of your fist. It's worth, say, half a billion dollars. This thing isn't just big, it's famous. Everyone wants to hold the diamond. They want to possess it.

You have one job: protect your fist-sized diamond. You can't let anyone steal it. You're not allowed to let anyone even touch it.

People want to take it from you. They'll do anything to get it. They tell you that the diamond isn't that important. They tell you that your diamond is just an old piece of coal and *their* diamond is the real thing. They tell you that your understanding of your diamond won't be complete until you listen to and believe what they believe about diamonds. They tell you that they've got a newer, better book about how to understand diamonds than you do. They even claim to know a newer, more accurate expert than you do.

How would you defend the diamond against these people? Write down three different defensive strategies below.

1. _____
2. _____
3. _____

Why Should I Defend My Faith?

What if you weren't protecting a diamond, but instead you were defending your faith? Would the strategies you wrote work?

Your faith is like a diamond. All kinds of people want to put their hands on your faith. They want to challenge it with their own tainted understanding of what the truth is. They want to hurt your faith by telling you that your truth isn't exactly true. Your job is to defend your faith. It's your job to stand up for the truth, to stand up for what you believe.

How do you do that? What do you need to be ready for? This week we'll be looking at Scripture and discussing how you can best defend your faith.

Live It Strong

- How strong are you at defending your faith?
- Why is defending your faith important?
- What can you do this week to learn how to better defend your faith?

God's Word

Then Peter got down out of the boat, walked on the water and came toward Jesus. But when he saw the wind, he was afraid and, beginning to sink, cried out, "Lord, save me!" Immediately Jesus reached out his hand and caught him. "You of little faith," he said, "why did you doubt?" Matthew 14:30–31

Now Thomas (called Didymus), one of the Twelve, was not with the disciples when Jesus came. So the other disciples told him, "We have seen the Lord!" But he said to them, "Unless I see the nail marks in his hands and put my finger where the nails were, and put my hand into his side, I will not believe it." A week later his disciples were in the house again, and Thomas was with them. Though the doors were locked, Jesus came and stood among them and said, "Peace be with you!" Then he said to Thomas, "Put your finger here; see my hands. Reach out your hand and put it into my side. Stop doubting and believe." Thomas said to him, "My Lord and my God!" John 20:24–28

If any of you lacks wisdom, he should ask God, who gives generously to all without finding fault, and it will be given to him. But when he asks, he must believe and not doubt, because he who doubts is like a wave of the sea, blown and tossed by the wind. James 1:5–6

Live It

It had to be the ultimate adventure.

Imagine getting yanked from your steady life of fishing, spending time with your family, and hanging out with your friends. Lured away with the promise of making a difference in the lives of others. Following the footsteps and lifestyle of the unknown young man who later claimed equality with God.

The disciples are hiding out in a home. They're living secretly. No one outside their small group knows where they are. They're hiding because Jesus has died and they're not sure what to do next. They're hiding because they could be arrested and killed like Jesus. They could be run out of town. With Jesus gone, they don't have any real defense.

Jesus first appears to the disciples and proves his existence. The Bible records that Jesus appeared to Thomas after appearing to the other disciples. I imagine that by the time Jesus appeared to Thomas, the doubter already had a long list of things Jesus would have to do to prove that he was the original, real, living Jesus. I imagine that Thomas's request was carefully calculated, but it was probably passionate, too. His desire to get an answer was fueled by his passion to see Jesus one more time.

Thomas wants proof. So he asks Jesus if he can touch his hands. I'd probably ask for the same kind of proof, wouldn't you? After all, it's not too much to ask for tangible evidence that this guy is who he says he is. Seeing Jesus isn't enough for Thomas; he wants to touch Jesus. Touching Jesus must have felt like a daring move to Thomas. In the end, Thomas's touching Jesus helps us understand a little more about Jesus' resurrected body, and it removes Thomas's doubt.

What doesn't rock about this story is that we don't know what Thomas does after this. Does he run around telling everyone? Does he write letters to believers about what he experienced? How does he express the fact that his doubt has changed to praise and his skepticism to confidence in solid proof?

Doubt's a real killer, isn't it? You think you know something, but you've got this nagging feeling. You want to believe it, but there's that nagging feeling again. Doubt can really wreck your belief. It can also ruin your ability to defend your faith. You get in a conversation with someone about your beliefs, but *you're* not sure beyond a doubt. That gets in the way of your ability to defend, explain, and prove what you believe about God. It gets in the way of the other person's understanding.

I think that Thomas's experience with Jesus' scars was the best proof Thomas had. After all, Thomas didn't ask to touch the face of Jesus; he wanted to touch his scars. The proof wasn't Thomas's having seen the face of Jesus, it was his seeing Jesus' scars. The same scars formed for Thomas's salvation were also his proof that Jesus was who he claimed to be.

How about you? Experienced Jesus' scars? Know about what he did for you? It's impossible to tell others about God unless you've walked to Jesus, fallen at his nail-scarred feet, and asked forgiveness. His broken body is both our eternal salvation and our proof.

Live It Strong

- Was it right for Thomas to want physical proof of Jesus' resurrection? Why?
- In what ways do you struggle with doubt?
- How does doubt ruin our ability to explain our faith to others?

God's Word

Surely you desire truth in the inner parts; you teach me wisdom in the inmost place. Psalm 51:6

And I will ask the Father, and he will give you another Counselor to be with you forever—the Spirit of truth. The world cannot accept him, because it neither sees him nor knows him. John 14:16–17

What may be known about God is plain to them, because God has made it plain to them. For since the creation of the world God's invisible qualities—his eternal power and divine nature—have been clearly seen, being understood from what has been made, so that men are without excuse. Romans 1:19–20

Live It

What is truth? You can define truth loads of ways. Here's some of the more popular ways people define truth.

According to Webster's dictionary, truth is "a transcendent fundamental or spiritual reality." That means that truth corresponds to an actual fact, a reality that you can't change, no matter how much you want to change it.

Some people say truth is how or what you feel. If something moves you emotionally, then that thing, or whatever moved you about that thing, is true. For example, say you like fluffy bears who live in trees. If those tree-living bears make you feel great, then you might believe that those bears are worth worshiping. You might decide to set up a cult that worships those bears. The divinity of those bears would be a truth.

Others might say that truth is what you make it or what you can think up, kind of like this: You can imagine that a planet exists where all the women are three feet taller than the men. Because your mind can think of such a place, that place must exist. It's a truth (to you) that planet exists.

Those are three different ways people try to explain or define truth. The problem is that none of them are completely right or fully describe the truth. In order to prove what truth really is, let's try some experi-

132

ments in our minds. We're doing them *only* in our brains because you shouldn't really do them. So for the sake of understanding truth, let's imagine the effects or results of the following experiments.

1. Imagine yourself getting a chair and throwing it as hard as you can against the wall. What happens? Easy to imagine, right? If you did that, you'd knock pictures off the wall, you'd put a hole in the wall, and you might break the chair. All of those are physical results of physical truth.
2. Imagine yourself staying up all night researching, writing, and typing an English paper (maybe you've actually done this). You've spent the night thinking and creating, so on top of being physically tired, you're mentally tired. What happens to your body? You're worn out, tired, and irritable. What happens to your mind? You can't think. You can't concentrate. You need sleep.

When you damage a wall with a chair or ruin your body with sleep deprivation, you are experiencing physical truth—what you do has actual effects on your wall or your body. Sometimes the best way to explain truth is to explain the effects of it.

Faith is often the same way. How do you explain faith in God? What can you say that will convince someone that God is real or that trusting him is okay? Sometimes the best proof is explaining what has happened to you. You can explain and define faith from the context of your experience. If you've experienced God, that's the basis for your explanation about him. How do you know that God exists? How can you define parts of God's personality and character? Through your experience. If you've experienced God's love and forgiveness, explaining that is the best way to explain him to someone who's interested in God.

Live It Strong

- Why do you think people interpret truth differently?
- Why is getting truth right so important?
- How easy is it for you to explain truth? How about your own faith?

God's Word

Then they called them in again and commanded them not to speak or teach at all in the name of Jesus. But Peter and John replied, "Judge for yourselves whether it is right in God's sight to obey you rather than God. For we cannot help speaking about what we have seen and heard." Acts 4:18–20

Then Agrippa said to Paul, "Do you think that in such a short time you can persuade me to be a Christian?" Paul replied, "Short time or long—I pray God that not only you but all who are listening to me today may become what I am, except for these chains." Acts 25:28–29 (read Acts 25:23–26:32 for the whole story)

But in your hearts set apart Christ as Lord. Always be prepared to give an answer to everyone who asks you to give the reason for the hope that you have. But do this with gentleness and respect. 1 Peter 3:15

Live It

Defending what you believe is never easy. But defending yourself in front of a ruler or someone who's intent on killing you or at least putting you in jail—that has to be the worst. Toward the end of his life, Paul faced more and more opportunities to defend his faith, to explain why he chose to believe in Christ, and to turn his back on his former job of persecuting Christians.

Acts 25 and 26 records Paul's standing up to major rulers of his time, specifically King Agrippa, who didn't agree with Paul and his devotion to Jesus. When you read the encounter between Paul and the king (Acts 25:23–26:32), you see these two guys get into a kind of verbal tug-of-war about what they believe. The highlight is reading what Paul says. Remember, Paul is standing before a major leader and in the presence of many people who don't agree with him at all. Read the passage now with that in mind.

What did you notice about Paul's defense? Below, write a few things you saw Paul do that you thought were really great.

_____

_____

_____

Why Should I
Defend My Faith?

I read the passage and made my own list. Here's four things I saw.

Paul is kind. The Bible mentions that Paul compliments Agrippa before he starts explaining himself. Later, as Paul is explaining himself, Festus (who's sitting in on the meeting) yells at Paul and tells him that he's nuts. Paul doesn't yell back. He maintains his composure.

Paul mentions his relationships and credentials. He bothers to tell who he knows, what he accomplished as a good Jew, and what he formerly believed. This is important. In order for Agrippa to understand why Paul is standing before him, he's got to understand how Paul used to live.

Paul clearly explains his conversion experience. Do you notice Paul trying to discuss theology with the king? He doesn't. He talks about the experience he's had with Jesus. No big words. No deep theology. He simply explains his own experience.

Paul appeals to Agrippa to believe the same way he does. I love that Paul doesn't try and offer Agrippa a formula or system for getting saved. Paul seems to say, "I've told you what I believe. I can't wait for the day when you believe it, too!"

When you look closely at Paul's explanation, you see a really cool example of how we ought to defend our faith to others: Keeping our cool. Talking about our former life. Explaining our experience with Jesus. Asking those listening to believe what we believe.

I don't know too many people who are really comfortable with defending their faith. Paul's example is clear and easy to follow, though. If we'd just tell others what we believe and let them make their decision, more people would be interested in Jesus and attracted to the same experience we've had.

Live It Strong

- Why do you think it was so easy for Paul to explain his faith?
- Which of the approaches Paul used in his defense is most important when sharing your faith—kindness, relationships, experience, or a call for a decision? Why?
- What have you learned from Paul's approach to defending his faith that you can use in your life?

God's Word

And the Lord's servant must not quarrel; instead, he must be kind to everyone, able to teach, not resentful. Those who oppose him he must gently instruct, in the hope that God will grant them repentance leading them to a knowledge of the truth. 2 Timothy 2:24–25

Whoever loves his brother lives in the light, and there is nothing in him to make him stumble. 1 John 2:10

Dear friends, let us love one another, for love comes from God. Everyone who loves has been born of God and knows God. 1 John 4:7

Live It

Defending your faith—it's like a boxing match sometimes, isn't it? You're in the middle of trying to explain what you believe to someone, and before long it turns into a verbal fight. You explain what you believe, and they fire back with a few "Yeah, buts" and their beliefs. Soon the two of you end up arguing. In those situations it can be tough to think clearly. So let's imagine a couple of situations and see if you can see a better way to defend your faith. After each story write down the pros and cons of what each person did.

The Donut Shop Confrontation

Mike invited his friends who go to another church to meet the two of you for breakfast today. You're not particularly fond of getting up early on a Saturday morning, but he said you should talk to these guys. When you show up, Mike is explaining the Trinity to them. You order your donuts and then sit and listen.

These guys don't seem to believe in the Trinity. After listening a bit longer, you're not sure that they believe in God at all—or at least in the same God you know, the one described in the Bible. They keep talking about Allah and using a Koran instead of the Bible you're used to.

Mike looks exasperated, so you try to offer a few more ideas. You begin with simple passages from the Old Testament, and the guys seem to be okay with your opinion. But when you get to the New Testament passages about Jesus being the only way to heaven and about the Holy Spirit, the guys begin to disagree with you. You let them talk, but you want to make a few points too. You try talking a little louder so they can hear you. Then they want to make a point, but you're almost shouting. So they have to shout a little louder to get you to hear them. Before long you are all yelling. The donut shop owner walks over and asks you to leave. Outside, you argue until they give up and walk away.

Pros: _____

Cons: _____

After the Ball Game

Lately it's been tough to hang out with Jane. You've known each other since first grade. She's always been there for you, and she's definitely your best friend. Last year the two of you attended a huge city-wide extreme sports skateboard thing put on by a friend's church. It had free pizza, really good music, and a message at the end. That night you became a Christian, but Jane didn't. Since then your relationship has been strained. You've been trying to think of a way to explain your faith to Jane a little better in the hopes that she'll make the same decision you did.

Tonight after the game you tried telling Jane about your beliefs. Not only does Jane not agree with you but she's weirdly defensive about it. You try to tell her about how you've changed, but Jane fires back with, "You don't seem any different to me!" You tell her that you're not angry about your parents' divorce anymore, but Jane says you're lying. She just keeps getting more and more angry. But you keep trying to explain what you believe and how you've changed. Eventually Jane storms off. Tonight was the worst fight the two of you have ever had.

Pros: _____

Cons: _____

Live It Strong

- Why is it important to listen to people when we're sharing our faith with them?
- Why do some people get really defensive when we tell them what we believe?
- How can we help others understand what we believe without offending them?

God's Word

When you are brought before synagogues, rulers and authorities, do not worry about how you will defend yourselves or what you will say, for the Holy Spirit will teach you at that time what you should say. Luke 12:11–12

Remember those earlier days after you had received the light, when you stood your ground in a great contest in the face of suffering. Sometimes you were publicly exposed to insult and persecution; at other times you stood side by side with those who were so treated. Hebrews 10:32–33

Dear friends, although I was very eager to write to you about the salvation we share, I felt I had to write and urge you to contend for the faith that was once for all entrusted to the saints. Jude 3

Live It

It's just a normal Saturday. You. A bag of chips. A tall glass of Coke. The TV remote. Your chores are done. You don't have to do anything. You don't have to be anywhere.

You. Snacks. Television.

Kings don't live this good.

Halfway through your favorite edited-for-television movie, the doorbell rings. You're not expecting anyone. You peek out the window. You don't know them, and you're not going to let them interrupt your movie.

Don't interrupt the king, you think to yourself.

After a few minutes the doorbell rings again, and it's followed by a knock, too. They're serious. Apparently, someone on the other side of the door really wants to talk to you. You mute the television and head for the door, frustrated and interrupted.

The guy on the other side of the screen reminds you of one of those caricature drawings. His smile is too big. His hair is too tall. You know what he's going to say milliseconds before his lips begin to flap. He's from the church on the north side of town, and he wants your soul in his church.

"Heeeelllooooo, young person. Are your parents home?"

Bzzzt. Begin auto blow-off mode.

"Uh, no sir. They'll be back later. You can come back later."

"Weeeellll then, young person, can I talk to you for a few minutes?"

Bzzzt. System update. Blow-off mode disengaging.

"Well, I was just spending some time . . ."

"All right. Great. I'm from the Lord's Castle. You've probably seen us in your neighborhood before. I don't think we've ever met. I've got some literature I'd like you to look at."

Bzzzt. Caution. System overload.

"Well, I'm kind of busy right now. Maybe when my parents . . ."

"Young person, are you aware of what happens to someone when they die? Do you realize that your body begins to rot and the only hope you have is being saved?"

"Actually, yeah. I know all about that."

"Fine, that's just fine. Do you realize that there's more to the Bible than what you've probably read? I've got something I want to show you. Our pastor had a revelation a few years ago, and God told him that the word he received was just as important and just as divine as the Bible you own. Could I interest you in a copy?"

Bzzzt. Note from system administrator. Get rid of this turkey.

"Okay."

"Honestly, young person, I'll need to explain this to you in more detail. Why don't I just step inside for a few minutes and we can talk further?"

Live It Strong

- If you were caught in this situation, what would you do?
- How do you defend what you believe to pushy people who want to cram their false beliefs down your throat?
- What have you learned this week that would help you defend your beliefs to this person?

God's Word

"You are my witnesses," declares the LORD, "and my servant whom I have chosen, so that you may know and believe me and understand that I am he. Before me no god was formed, nor will there be one after me." Isaiah 43:10

And the Lord's servant must not quarrel; instead, he must be kind to everyone, able to teach, not resentful. Those who oppose him he must gently instruct, in the hope that God will grant them repentance leading them to a knowledge of the truth. 2 Timothy 2:24–25

But in your hearts set apart Christ as Lord. Always be prepared to give an answer to everyone who asks you to give the reason for the hope that you have. But do this with gentleness and respect. 1 Peter 3:15

Live It

Ever wondered exactly how you'd defend your faith to someone who didn't believe in God? If you've never had the experience of defending your faith, when the moment comes where you actually *have* to defend it, you can get flustered. Explaining what you believe is too important to get a brain freeze at the wrong moment. Imagine trying to explain to someone how they could win a billion dollars. You wouldn't want to mess that up, right? If you were at the top of a burning building and had to explain how to get off the building to a group of people trapped with you, you wouldn't want to mess that up, right? Being able to explain and defend your faith is a jillion times more important than those things.

If being able to explain your faith is that important, then it's important to practice explaining it. Try this. Get a friend and give them the following scenario: He or she is a non-Christian friend you've known for over a year. You've decided to tell your unsaved friend about what you believe. Tell your (real) friend that you're going to explain what you believe, and he or she should put down everything you believe. Each of you should do your best to defend your belief. Try not to argue or get too angry with each other.

Why Should I
Defend My Faith?

When you're done, talk about how each of you did, but especially how you did. Ask your friend to help you evaluate how well you defended your faith. When you're done discussing, write down a few things you've learned from trying this.

_____

_____

_____

_____

What did you learn? Was explaining your faith as easy as you thought it would be? Was it more difficult than you'd imagined? Look, it's not always easy to explain or defend your faith. In fact, if your friends or even your parents were honest, they'd tell you that defending their faith freaks them out. Yeah, it's not easy.

So how can you get more comfortable defending what you believe? Actually you've just practiced the most helpful step you could ever learn. Look, you can spend years in a classroom learning the fine points of faith-debating, and that might be okay. But until you actually practice defending your faith, you haven't learned the most important aspect: practice, practice, practice. That's the best way to learn the fine art of defending your faith.

Live It Strong

- What have you learned about defending your faith from this activity?
- Using what you've learned from this activity, how would you help a friend better understand how to defend their faith?
- How can you apply what you've learned about defending your faith from this illustration and from Scripture to your life?

141

WHY SHOULD I LOVE MY PARENTS?

God's Word

Honor your father and your mother, so that you may live long in the land the LORD your God is giving you. Exodus 20:12

Listen, my son, to your father's instruction and do not forsake your mother's teaching. They will be a garland to grace your head and a chain to adorn your neck. Proverbs 1:8–9

Children, obey your parents in everything, for this pleases the Lord. Colossians 3:20

Live It

Your parents can do some strange things, can't they? Do they stress out over the strangest things? Do they argue over silly things? Does one tell you to do one thing and the other tell you to do something completely different?

Some days it doesn't take much to freak out your parents. But you already know that. I bet you already know that sometimes the littlest thing can make your parents act like aliens. Ever watched your parents go from normal to abnormal in under three seconds? Watched them totally lose it? On the lines below, write three of the strangest things your parents have done:

1. _____
_____

2. _____
_____

3. _____
_____

Yeah, your parents can do some weird things. But in spite of their weirdness, you've gotta love them. Not "gotta love them" because the Bible says you have to so much as you've got to love them because they gave life to you. They've cared for you. They've clothed and fed

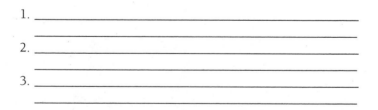

Why Should I
Love My Parents?

you. And sometimes all of that care for you has led them to kind of lose their minds.

How do you love your parents? What can you do to show that you love them? Why is it so difficult to love them?

This week we're conquering your parents. You can love them in amazing ways in spite of their weirdness. As you live out this week, consider doing the following things for your parents:

- pray for them every morning
- say good morning to them when they wake you up every morning this week
- tell them you love them each day this week
- do kind things for them without having to be asked to do them
- work to get along with your siblings all week so you won't stress your parents out by fighting
- ask them their advice about a huge issue in your life
- do your homework without them reminding you to do it

This week your challenge is to totally and completely love your parents. Along the way we'll talk about how to love, obey, and honor your parents in everything you do.

Live It Strong

- Rate yourself: How good are you at letting your parents know you love them?
- Why is it important to let your parents know that you love and appreciate them?
- What can you do this week to help your parents know how much you appreciate them?

145

God's Word

Listen, my son, to your father's instruction and do not forsake your mother's teaching. Proverbs 1:8

Listen, my sons, to a father's instruction; pay attention and gain understanding. I give you sound learning, so do not forsake my teaching. When I was a boy in my father's house, still tender, and an only child of my mother, he taught me and said, "Lay hold of my words with all your heart; keep my commands and you will live." Proverbs 4:1–4

Children, obey your parents in the Lord, for this is right. "Honor your father and mother"—which is the first commandment with a promise— "that it may go well with you and that you may enjoy long life on the earth." Ephesians 6:1–3

Live It

Can you wrap a word up in a ball and roll it around? Sometimes it's good to just think about a word and see what happens, what ideas come to mind, and what concepts pop up. So I'd like you to let a word roll around in your head for a bit. Here's the word. Ready?

Honor.

Give it a few minutes. Let the word sit in your head. When you're ready, I'd like you to write down a few words or phrases that came to your mind as you thought of that word. Write them down below.

_____

_____

_____

Why talk about honor?

When you read what the Bible says about how kids are supposed to treat their parents, the word *honor* jumps out at you. Over and over, the Bible tells kids to honor their parents.

Ephesians 6:1–3 is a great passage because it's limited in what it says. It doesn't give us many options for how we can to treat our parents. I like that. There's not much wiggle room. Ephesians simply uses that great word, *honor,* when it tells how we're supposed to treat our parents.

Why Should I
Love My Parents?

How can you define that word? Today, honor is usually reserved for some pretty important things. For example:

- You honor the president of the United States. When he arrives and as he's leaving, he's honored with a band and with soldiers standing at attention.
- You honor great musicians. When they're done performing, you give them a standing ovation. When they arrive in town to sign CDs and posters at a record store, people honor them by bringing them gifts and lining up around the store.
- You honor your grandparents because they're old and wise. How do you honor grandparents? You listen to them. You're quiet when they talk. You take them seriously.

The word *honor* is a significant word, and I think that's why the Bible uses it. God wants us to remember the place that our parents are supposed to have in our lives. Because we see them every day, it's easy to take our parents for granted. It's easy to treat everything they say and do lightly and not take them seriously. But God's Word tells us to honor our parents. God wants us to treat them like they're visiting royalty. He wants us to give them the same honor that we would give our favorite music star. He wants us to pay attention to them like they're wise and experienced.

With honor comes obeying, respecting, and listening. If we're not listening to our parents and taking their words seriously, we're not treating them the way God wants us to. If we're not obeying our parents, we're not obeying God. And if we're not honoring our parents, then we're living opposite of the way that God asks us to live.

Today, honor your parents. Treat them like they're a rock star. When your dad comes home from work, ask him for his autograph. Over dinner, ask your parents for their advice about something, and then listen to what they say and act on their advice. Later in the evening, ask your parents to tell you a few stories about their childhood. Today, do everything you can to make your parents feel honored, loved, and respected.

147

Live It Strong

- Why is it important to honor your parents?
- How do your parents make it difficult to honor them?
- What can you do today to honor your parents?

God's Word

Remember your Creator in the days of your youth. Ecclesiastes 12:1

For God said, "Honor your father and mother" and "Anyone who curses his father or mother must be put to death." Matthew 15:4

Flee the evil desires of youth, and pursue righteousness, faith, love and peace, along with those who call on the Lord out of a pure heart. 2 Timothy 2:22

Live It

I wish I had an awesome history with my parents. After all, if someone's going to write a section in a book to try to help other people with living with their parents, that person ought to at least have a good history with their own parents, right? If I'm going to write about loving your parents, I ought to have been a good kid. Well, I hope this doesn't burst your bubble, but I was an awful kid. When I was younger I treated my parents really, really badly. I could tell you all kinds of awful kid stories. The night I yelled at my dad in the middle of the public library. The time I made my mom cry about a guy she was dating. Or the time I yelled at her in front of her boss at work.

The time I treated my mom the worst was probably the time I tried to tape record myself calling my mom a bad name. A really, really bad name.

I had this friend who didn't get along with his parents. Really, I guess you could say that none of my group of friends got along with our parents very well. But this guy *really* didn't get along with his parents. His anger at his parents fueled all of us who hung out with him to fight with our parents. He fought, so we fought. Fighting with your parents was contagious. I'm not sure how the idea started, but one of us had the idea of putting together a tape recording of each of us yelling at our parents or calling them a really bad name. The plan was that we would each get a tape recorder and do our best to make our parents really mad. Then in the middle of the fight, when we were yelling back

148

and forth with our parents, we'd turn on the tape recorder, let out an awful word, and then run and hide in our rooms. We'd get together the next day, compare our tapes, and laugh like crazy.

The night I tried to do this, I completely messed it up. When I tried to tape record myself calling my mom a really bad name, I accidentally pushed play instead. The tape in the tape recorder had some music for children on it, so Old MacDonald came blasting out. I dropped the thing and ran to my room. My mom followed after me, and I got a huge spanking.

That's awful, isn't it? I've recently apologized to my mom for this stupid moment in my younger years. What a dork, huh? What kind of kid tries to be mean to their mom, then tries to tape record their mom getting mad just to impress their friends? Maybe you've never been this mean, but have you ever done something mean to your parents on purpose? Have you ever done something to them just to hurt their feelings or acted awful just because you were in a bad mood?

All of us have caused pain in our parents' lives. We've all been difficult to live with, and we've all hurt our parents' feelings. If you've been awful and been difficult to live with, you've gotta go to your parents and ask for forgiveness. When I asked my mom to forgive me for acting so stupid with the tape recorder, she laughed, hugged me, and told me that she remembered but that she also forgave me. I felt awful reminding my mom of what a jerk I was, but I felt a lot better when I realized that even though I hurt her, my mom was willing to forgive me.

If you've been awful to live with and if you've hurt your parents feelings, I bet that they'd be willing to forgive you. I imagine that when you go to your parents and ask forgiveness they'll be willing to hug you and forgive you. Drudging up old junk and asking for forgiveness isn't easy, but if you want a good relationship with your parents, you've got to do it. Today, go to your parents and ask them to forgive you for the silly, hurtful things you've done. If you're brave enough to try this, your relationship with them will get stronger.

Live It Strong

- Is it difficult for you to be kind to your parents? Why?
- When have you had to ask forgiveness of your parents?
- What makes asking forgiveness from your parents difficult?

God's Word

Better a poor but wise youth than an old but foolish king who no longer knows how to take warning. Ecclesiastes 4:13

For God said, "Honor your father and mother" and "Anyone who curses his father or mother must be put to death." Matthew 15:4

Children, obey your parents in the Lord, for this is right. Ephesians 6:1

Live It

Do you love your parents? You probably do. Do they know it?

Since the Bible commands us to love and respect our parents, it's up to us to live out that command. How do you do that? How do you live out God's command to love, respect, and show kindness to your parents? How do you help your parents know that you love them without being overly sappy? Here are some ideas.

Clean your room. Your parents will understand that you take what they've given you seriously when you take care of your personal possessions. I know it sounds kind of weird, but the more you take care of your stuff, the more your parents understand that you love them. When you clean your room without them having to ask, they know that you love and respect them.

Do your chores. No doubt your parents have given you a list of things that they want you to do each week. Do you ever skip those chores? Do you ever fight with your parents about doing those chores? A great way to show your parents that you love and respect them is to do your chores without complaining. Do your chores, and consider even getting them done early.

Do their chores. Your parents have things they have to do around the house every day. If they're not too huge and if your parents will let you, do their chores, too. An even better approach is to watch the chores that your parents do every week and do them without telling them that you're going to do them. Your parents will be surprised when they discover that you're doing their chores, and they'll feel incredibly loved and respected.

Obey them. Do you ever fight with your parents about things they don't want you to do? Do you ever fight with them because they've asked you to do something and you don't want to do it? Obeying your parents is not always easy. The toughest part of obeying your parents is putting your desires and plans on hold and doing what they've asked.

Practice kindness. Every day your parents face really tough things. Their jobs. Responsibilities. Life. They need someone in their corner supporting and encouraging them. This might sound silly, but your kindness to them can carry them along when their lives seem too difficult. When you love your parents and you are kind to them, it motivates them to keep going, and it motivates them to do great things for you.

So the big question isn't what you should do to help your parents. It's not even what the Bible says about how you should treat your parents ('cause we talked about that yesterday, right?). The big question is, How will you love your parents today? Which of your chores or their chores will you do right now to show your parents that you really do care and really do love them? How will you obey them today?

The Bible has a lot to say about how we should treat our parents. Our responsibility is to act on what the Bible says. If we love God and our parents, we've got to do it. We love our parents because we want to love and obey God.

Live It Strong

- Why is it important to encourage your parents?
- Which of these ways to show love would be the most difficult for you? Why?
- What would happen to your relationship with your parents if you followed the advice in this devotion?

151

God's Word

A new command I give you: Love one another. As I have loved you, so you must love one another. By this all men will know that you are my disciples, if you love one another. John 13:34–35

Let us therefore make every effort to do what leads to peace and to mutual edification. Romans 14:19

And let us consider how we may spur one another on toward love and good deeds. Hebrews 10:24

Live It

I'd like to make a request. We should get a manual about how to live with and love our parents when we are born. Okay, maybe not when we're born . . . maybe when we're teenagers. We need tools to raise parents. I know that you've probably heard that teenagers are tough to raise and that your parents wish they had a book to help raise you.

I don't agree. I think *we* need the book to help us raise our parents. I know this because of my parents. I'm sure your parents do some nutty things. Have they ever embarrassed you? Have they ever done something in public or in front of your friends that made you want to say, "Uhh, no, dude, those aren't my parents"? Mine have.

Once when I was younger, my mom and I were at my brother's wedding. Where we're from, they don't just have a wedding and then a nice dessert table. They have a sit-down dinner. They have a gift-opening ceremony. They have the presentation of the bride, groom, their wedding party, and everyone that's remotely related to the couple. It ends up being a long, drawn-out thing. Usually at this kind of party there's music, and often, when the mood is right and the people plan it, someone dances. These are usually good moments of celebration. And usually the people dancing know how to dance. Usually they're good at it.

At my brother's wedding they didn't have dancing—well, I mean, they weren't *supposed* to have dancing. In order to have some kind of entertainment during the dinner, my brother asked a friend who played the accordion to wander around the room and play for people. This guy could play the accordion. I know, because I typically dislike accordion music, so if I thought it was good, then he must have been a great player. The guy was cool and what he was playing was okay. But when he came over and played near my mom, things got a little out of hand.

I didn't know it at the time, but my mom really likes accordion music. The player came over, and my mom couldn't resist. The music slowly took over my mom. First her head began to bob up and down. Then her whole body bobbed. She began to pick up her legs. Before long my mom was moving and reacting to the music. Even worse, the accordion player began to react to my mom's dancing. He began to dance, and my mom started dancing around him. With her bobbing up and down and trotting around him and him doing turns and twists around her (while still playing), you'd have thought *they* had just gotten married.

Sometimes your parents do embarrassing things. This was a major embarrassing moment for me. Watching your mom dance can be like watching the before, during, and after of a train wreck. You know something awful is going to happen, but you can't stop it.

I don't know what you're supposed to do when your parents embarrass themselves—and you. That's why I'd like a manual on how to raise parents. I think the best thing to do when your parents do embarrassing things is to just love them. You can't change them, and you can't move out. But you can love them. Yeah, your parents will do silly things. They're going to wear clothes that aren't up-to-date and don't match. They're going to use words that make them sound like dorks. They're going to ask you embarrassing questions in front of your friends. When they do, your best move is to love them. When they do stuff like that in public, let them know you love them, right in public and right at the moment when they embarrass themselves. When you do that, your parents will feel loved, and they'll listen when you help them understand how they embarrassed themselves, too.

Oh, and just a word of caution. If you're at a wedding with your mom and she likes accordion music, act like you're sick and make her take you home. You'll be glad you did. I promise.

153

Live It Strong

- When have your parents embarrassed you? What did you do?
- Why do our parents embarrass us?
- How should you respond to your parents when they do things you think are strange?

God's Word

*Each of you must respect his mother and father, and you must observe my
Sabbaths. I am the LORD your God. Leviticus 19:3*

*Listen to your father, who gave you life, and do not despise your mother
when she is old. Proverbs 23:22*

*Children, obey your parents in the Lord, for this is right. "Honor your
father and mother"—which is the first commandment with a promise—
"that it may go well with you and that you may enjoy long life on the
earth." Ephesians 6:1–3*

Live It

This is a pretty typical day for your dad. He's been to work, and it
wasn't a great day there. When it's been a bad day at work, it's usually a
bad night at home. Bad days at work mean that Dad yells at everyone for
no reason. Tonight isn't any different. It begins when the door slams.
Bang!

> You: "Hey, Dad. How was your day?"
>
> Dad: [Grunt.]
>
> You: "Dad, could I have my allowance now? I've done all
>   my chores."
>
> Dad: "Chores? You have no idea what chores are. *You* try
>   spending a day at work where I work. *You* spend your
>   life answering to a boss that looks at you like you're an
>   ant. You do that and *then* we'll talk about chores and
>   your allowance."

154

You know it's best to just let dad be. He's angry, and it's best not to
upset him too much.

Later, at dinner, your dad is still angry. And with the entire family
walking on eggshells and trying not to upset him, it's a very quiet dinner. Quiet until your sister drops a forkful of food, that is.

Your sister:	"Yikes. Sorry!"
Mom:	"It's okay, sweetie. Do you need a paper towel? Can you please pick up the food off the floor?"
Your sister:	"I've got it, Mom. Thanks."
Dad:	"When I was a kid and I dropped a fork, my dad would make me eat with my hands. Should I make you eat with your hands? I think I should."

Just then your dad grabs the fork out of your sister's hand and begins yelling, "Eat with your hands!" at the top of his lungs.

| Mom: | "Honey, she's had a hard day. It was just an accident." |
| Dad: | "You want to know about having a hard day? I'll tell you about hard days. I work every day. I come home tired every day. I slave for you people. How do you show your thanks? You throw silverware and smart off at me. All of you better begin to show me more respect and be more appreciative of what I do around here. Period." |

The entire family ate in silence for the rest of the meal.

Live It Strong

- What advice would you give a friend caught in this situation?
- Are there ever times when you shouldn't honor your parents? When?
- What have you learned this week that would help you honor your parents in this kind of situation?

155

God's Word

Each of you must respect his mother and father, and you must observe my Sabbaths. I am the LORD your God. Leviticus 19:3

If I speak in the tongues of men and of angels, but have not love, I am only a resounding gong or a clanging cymbal. 1 Corinthians 13:1

If anyone does not provide for his relatives, and especially for his immediate family, he has denied the faith and is worse than an unbeliever. 1 Timothy 5:8

Live It

Have you ever thought about how difficult your parents' job is? They work. They take care of the house. They take care of you. But your parents' job is so much more than caring for you or paying the bills. They also support you. They go to your games and your recitals. Have you ever stopped to thank them for what they do? Do you ever take time to let your parents know that you appreciate everything they do for you?

It's not always easy to express your thanks to your parents. It can be difficult to know exactly what your parents go through each day and exactly how they help you with everything you do.

So try this. Arrange with your parents to be the parent for a day. Choose a Saturday and ask your parents to let you do anything they'd usually do on a Saturday, like yard work, paying the bills, and running errands. As you're doing your parents' chores and taking care of their business, write down some of the unusual things you're experiencing. Write down how it feels to do your parents' work for them. If you're feeling stressed with too many things to do or if you're wondering how you'd solve some problems, write that down, too.

When you're done running their errands and acting like you're them for a day, get a sheet of paper, crayons or markers, and other things that you might use to make your parents a card. Think up and create a card for your parents that represents your thankfulness for them and your respect for them for doing all the things that they do for you. You might want to write some things that express how you felt while you were pretending to be them for the day. You can use the list you created throughout the day as a reference.

When you've created the card, present it to your parents. Give it to them and thank them for what they do for you every day. Thank them for taking care of you, for going to your special events, and for being there when you need support and encouragement.

Live It Strong

- What have you learned this week about loving your parents?
- Using what you've learned this week, how would you help a friend better understand how to love their parents better?
- How can you apply what you've learned about your relationship with your parents from this illustration and from Scripture to your life?

157

WHY
ARE EMOTIONS
SO
FRUSTRATING?

God's Word

A fool shows his annoyance at once, but a prudent man overlooks an insult. Proverbs 12:16

Do not be quickly provoked in your spirit, for anger resides in the lap of fools. Ecclesiastes 7:9

"In your anger do not sin": Do not let the sun go down while you are still angry. Ephesians 4:26

Live It

You've had it.

No matter what you do, nothing makes you feel okay. You've tried getting more rest, but that doesn't work. You've tried relaxing; no dice. Last weekend you stayed home and watched movies. Nothing seems to work.

You're sad all the time. Nothing makes you happy. The test you got back last week? You did great, but the one question you missed made you angry. You got nominated to be president of the French Club, but you were upset that more people didn't vote for you.

You've never really felt like this before. You're not usually this angry or this sad. Emotionally, physically, and every other way, nothing seems right. You feel totally and completely uncomfortable in every way. You even wish you could crawl out of your own skin. Nothing you feel seems right. Nothing you do seems right.

Maybe you've had a day like this, where you felt uncomfortable in your skin. Maybe you've felt like nothing you could feel was right. And maybe you've had a day when you've responded to everything you encounter with emotions you never thought you had in you.

We've all been there. We've experienced days when our skin doesn't seem to fit, we can't keep control of our emotions, and we lash out at anyone who comes close. It doesn't even have to be something specific, does it? Sometimes we just feel nasty, bad, icky—and we can't figure out why. On the lines below, write about the last time you felt

Why Are Emotions
So Frustrating?

that way. What emotions were you experiencing? How did you feel? What did you do?

_____
_____
_____
_____

If you've been there, then this week is for you. If you've experienced emotions you don't know how to deal with, then you know how difficult it feels to try to understand your own emotions and not react poorly because you feel rotten. Take time to ask God to use this week to help you learn the power of your emotions and the way he wants you to control them.

Live It Strong

- Why is handling our emotions correctly important?
- What things in your life seem to test you emotionally?
- How can you rely on God this week to help you handle your emotions?

God's Word

I, even I, am he who comforts you. Who are you that you fear mortal men, the sons of men, who are but grass, that you forget the LORD your Maker, who stretched out the heavens and laid the foundations of the earth, that you live in constant terror every day because of the wrath of the oppressor, who is bent on destruction? Isaiah 51:12–13

Do not be quickly provoked in your spirit, for anger resides in the lap of fools. Ecclesiastes 7:9

My dear brothers, take note of this: Everyone should be quick to listen, slow to speak and slow to become angry. James 1:19

Live It

God's Word can feel so cold and lifeless, can't it? I don't mean to take away from God's Word. It's powerful. It's authoritative. It's without error. Still, sometimes reading the Bible and the stories in it over and over so much can take away from the coolness of the stories. After we read them so often, the stories and even the truth can seem flat and without excitement.

But have you ever noticed the emotions in God's Word? Ever noticed the really frustrating emotions many of God's people dealt with? His Word is packed with moments when good people had arguments, disappointments, problems, and frustrations. Sometimes these people took these tough emotions and made huge mistakes. For example:

- Moses got emotional and broke the Ten Commandments (Exod. 32:1–20).
- Paul and Barnabas argued over John Mark (Acts 15:36–41).
- Saul tried to kill David (1 Sam. 19:1–24).

Those people are in God's Word. Many of them were looked up to by other believers. They were leaders. And they all dealt with very difficult emotions. They had awful moments, fights, outbursts, and other things you'd never expect from people in God's Word. It's weird to think of people in the Bible having bad, overemotional moments, but that's exactly what those passages tell us. God's people aren't always perfect. They're not always able to control their tongues. Sometimes they fight. Sometimes they're incredibly human.

What does that mean for you and me?

If those people who were respected and did great things for God had to work through and experience difficult emotions, you will, too.

Sometimes when you're arguing with a friend, feeling depressed, or freaking out, you feel completely alone. It's like you're the only person who has ever experienced an awful moment or fought with someone. When you're feeling awful, you also feel like you're not a Christian because someone who says they love God could never experience these kinds of emotions, right? No, that's not true. Following God means following him with everything we are—bad emotions and fights with our friends included. That's why God's Word is so cool. It doesn't just tell you how to live, it shows you how people who love God have lived and how they've failed.

Feeling weird? Experiencing emotions you don't know how to deal with? Fighting with your friends, your parents, or your teachers? Embarrassing yourself with uncontrolled emotional outbursts?

You're not abnormal. You're not ungodly. You are you, just like God made you. God loves you just the way you are—emotions and all.

Live It Strong

- Why is it easy to react poorly to negative emotions?
- Does it help knowing that people in Scripture dealt with tough emotions? How?
- Why is it important to remember that it's okay to not be perfect?

God's Word

Redeem me from the oppression of men, that I may obey your precepts.
Psalm 119:134

This is what the Sovereign LORD says: You have gone far enough, O princes of Israel! Give up your violence and oppression and do what is just and right. Stop dispossessing my people, declares the Sovereign LORD. Ezekiel 45:9

But he said to me, "My grace is sufficient for you, for my power is made perfect in weakness." Therefore I will boast all the more gladly about my weaknesses, so that Christ's power may rest on me. That is why, for Christ's sake, I delight in weaknesses, in insults, in hardships, in persecutions, in difficulties. For when I am weak, then I am strong. 2 Corinthians 12:9–10

Live It

Big brothers can be the worst of God's creations, can't they? If you have a big brother, then you know what I'm talking about. When you're at your worst, your annoying big brother always seems to be there to antagonize you and make your life worse. If you have an antagonistic, mean, and abnormally rude older brother then you know what kind of brother I was.

I was an awful older brother for my sister. Alison was a very sweet, kind younger sister. Every day after school I'd come home and make it my sole ambition to terrorize Alison. I'd use whatever I could find to scare her and make her miserable. I'd grab the silly things our parents left on tables for decorations and threaten to hit her with them. Usually I'd start chasing her, she'd run, and I'd keep chasing her. This usually lasted until one of us got hurt (it was usually her), until my mom got home and I got in trouble, or until my sister was able to make it into her room and lock the door before I could catch her. I could terrorize my little sister for just a few minutes or for an hour.

We've both grown up. (Well, actually only Alison has grown up. I still chase my kids around the house almost every day, but at least I don't terrorize them with small objects.) When we get together Alison and I often joke about the times when I terrorized her. She usually laughs, and I usually apologize to her for the things I did. Once in a while I still feel bad about what I did to her. No brother who loves his sister should do those kind of things.

Some things in life are like that, aren't they? Things that seek to chase you. I'm not trying to overspiritualize the abuse that I gave my sister. But if you think about it, each day we live we seem to face things that try to push our buttons and try to make us upset. Sometimes life seems to like playing with our emotions. It doesn't have to be any one thing. Sometimes you just get in a bad mood. Sometimes getting less sleep than you need can make you feel rotten. This stuff can make you feel like everything is chasing after you and trying to hurt you.

I think that God allows us to face those things to help us understand how emotionally strong we are. I also think that God allows those kind of tests to help us see how he wants to make us emotionally whole. When life seems to be conspiring against us, when everything seems to be testing us emotionally, and when our only hope for keeping ourselves together is God, then we've learned who is really in our corner and who really loves us.

When things push our emotional buttons, when it feels like they're chasing us around the house and terrorizing us, God is there. Whatever you feel is chasing you right now, you need to remember that God wants to protect you. He can't stand for you to be attacked, and he wants to keep you from being hurt.

Live It Strong

- What things in your life chase your emotions around?
- When we feel attacked, how does God protect us?
- Why does God protect us when we feel attacked?

God's Word

Why is life given to a man whose way is hidden, whom God has hedged in? For sighing comes to me instead of food; my groans pour out like water. What I feared has come upon me; what I dreaded has happened to me. I have no peace, no quietness; I have no rest, but only turmoil. Job 3:23–26

If the only home I hope for is the grave, if I spread out my bed in darkness, if I say to corruption, "You are my father," and to the worm, "My mother" or "My sister," where then is my hope? Who can see any hope for me? Will it go down to the gates of death? Will we descend together into the dust? Job 17:13–16

But as for me, I watch in hope for the LORD, I wait for God my Savior; my God will hear me. Micah 7:7

Live It

Knowing how to handle yourself in tough moments isn't always easy. When life seems really weird it can be hard to know what to do with your weird emotions. Here are a few emotionally difficult situations. Check them out and write what you'd do to correctly handle your emotions.

1. *The bad mood.* You woke up today in a *bad* mood. It's actually been days since you were in a good mood, and you're not sure why. Anyway, all day you've been snapping at everyone. You yelled at your mom for not stopping at the right entrance when she dropped you off at school. You argued with your biology teacher about an assignment. You even argued with one of the lunchroom ladies about the food. On the way home you yelled at your best friend. She yelled back and the two of you argued back and forth the entire way home. You parted with "Great, I'm never talking to you again either."

What do you do when you've allowed your negative emotions to ruin a good relationship?

_____

_____

_____

Why Are Emotions
So Frustrating?

2. *The big rejection.* You're majorly in love with Kendra. You've known her since sixth grade, but since then she's gotten really beautiful. You don't just like her, you *like her.* At school you always try to catch her in the hall. You know where her classes are, and you casually wait outside the room hoping she'll see you. When she sees you she usually says hi. Her "hi" means a lot to you, and you read it like she likes you.

So today you decided to go for it and tell her what you think about her. You went to her locker and told her that you like her and want to go out with her. Her response was a big, fat, "Nah, I don't date geeks." Now you feel worthless, completely uncool, and very ugly.

Is it okay to let someone else make you feel bad about yourself? How should you handle your emotions when someone you like turns you down?

_____

_____

_____

3. *Just let me stay in bed.* You wouldn't say that you're depressed, you just have no desire to get out of bed. You're not sad. You're not suicidal. You're not angry or hiding from your parents. You just don't want to get out of bed.

Yesterday after school you went to your room and didn't feel like leaving. You've been here in bed for a day. You're not planning on going to church tomorrow, and you're thinking about playing sick and skipping school on Monday. Your parents are worried. They think you're acting too sad and too weird.

Is this depression? Is it okay to never want to leave your room? How should you deal with emotions like these?

_____

_____

_____

_____

Live It Strong

- Which of these situations is most like your life?
- Why do our emotions sometimes rule us?
- What happens when we allow our emotions to control us?

Week Ten

God's Word

O LORD, do not rebuke me in your anger or discipline me in your wrath. For your arrows have pierced me, and your hand has come down upon me. Psalm 38:1–2

For I am about to fall, and my pain is ever with me. I confess my iniquity; I am troubled by my sin. Many are those who are my vigorous enemies; those who hate me without reason are numerous. Psalm 38:17–19

O LORD, do not forsake me; be not far from me, O my God. Come quickly to help me, O Lord my Savior. Psalm 38:21–22

Live It

Have you ever read through the Psalms? I know, it's a huge book, it's in the Old Testament, and those two facts alone can make the book feel really useless to read. But if you check the book out you'll notice that the book contains a huge amount of heart. Psalms is a very human book, full of honest emotion and lots of lessons on how to live life and glorify God.

Part of that honesty includes some of David's true feelings when his whole world seems to be imploding. Sometimes David blames his pain on an attacker. Other times David knows his pain is the result of his own sin. Psalm 38 paints an amazing picture of how he reacts when he's feeling attacked and abused. Take a minute to read that psalm.

Did you notice the emotion David expresses in that psalm? Did you hear how attacked he felt? Did you notice how in the midst of his attacked feelings David feels like he's been forgotten by God? Here's a few things I saw as I read David's words.

Verses 1–11: David doesn't mince words about what has caused his pain, and he is honest about how he feels. David's sin has caused the pain he's experiencing. But David is experiencing more than the effects of his sin. He's being attacked. His body is failing. Because of his sin and his physical and emotional pain, his friends are avoiding him. Has

this ever happened to you? You've messed up, you're feeling rotten, and so your friends start avoiding you? No fun, huh?

Verses 12–16: David feels absolutely helpless. He describes himself as someone who can't speak or hear. His emotions have taken him to a place where he feels so helpless that he can't act. Have you ever felt like you're so stuck in something awful that you can't make a right move? Ever felt like you can't make a right decision?

Verses 17–22: David doubts his ability to keep going. His pain, rejection, and feeling of being forgotten by God have taken over his emotions. David doesn't just feel forgotten, he feels attacked and believes that God doesn't care about him. Have you ever felt that way? Ever felt that you're not just suffering, you're suffering alone? That feeling is enough to throw your emotions into overdrive. It can cause you to snap at people you love and to lash out at strangers.

I find it a huge help to read about how someone has had to deal with their own mistakes and their own feelings of being abandoned by friends and by God. Have you ever felt the effects of your own sin? Have you ever felt that God had forgotten you? Those things can cause you to feel really emotionally drained. And that emotionally drained feeling can cause you to make some bad mistakes. You end up fighting with people. You start to turn your back on God. Your life can go down the drain in every way.

When I feel that way, I like to remember David. He wrote these words because his life was, at times, a wreck. Later on, David got his life together. That's our hope. When we're feeling like we've been forgotten by God and our emotions are going over the edge, we have hope. If we continue to try to focus on God and follow him, our emotions will calm down, and we'll begin to feel better. And eventually, we'll feel okay.

Live It Strong

- When have you felt attacked by someone or something?
- Why do you think God allowed David's doubts and fears to be included in the Bible?
- Which of these sections of verses can you most relate to? Why?

God's Word

I am worn out from groaning; all night long I flood my bed with weeping and drench my couch with tears. My eyes grow weak with sorrow; they fail because of all my foes. Away from me, all you who do evil, for the LORD has heard my weeping. The LORD has heard my cry for mercy; the LORD accepts my prayer. Psalm 6:6–9

Save me, O God, for the waters have come up to my neck. I sink in the miry depths, where there is no foothold. I have come into the deep waters; the floods engulf me. I am worn out calling for help; my throat is parched. My eyes fail, looking for my God. Psalm 69:1–3

What misery is mine! I am like one who gathers summer fruit at the gleaning of the vineyard; there is no cluster of grapes to eat, none of the early figs that I crave. . . . But as for me, I watch in hope for the LORD, I wait for God my Savior; my God will hear me. Micah 7:1, 7

Live It

You know Elise gets emotional, but her constant crying is really getting out of control. She hasn't always been like this. Years ago you and Elise got to know each other at camp, and you've been great friends ever since. Last year Elise went with your family on vacation. Sometimes you still look through the pictures together and laugh.

But over the past several months, Elise has changed. She's not the fun person that she always was. She cries over anything. For example,

- last week she cried when she missed one question on her algebra quiz
- yesterday she lost it when she heard that they were changing the cheerleading uniforms
- today she bawled for a half hour because she forgot to pack a drink in her lunch

Why Are Emotions So Frustrating?

After today's emotional meltdown you offered to walk home from school with her. As you started walking, you decided to ask her about her constant crying. You begin.

"Elise, what's going on? Why do you cry about everything?"

At just the mention of her crying, her eyes tear up, and it's downhill from there. She stays quiet. She wipes her nose and dabs at her eyes with her sleeve. The two of you walk in silence for a half a block. Then Elise stops and begins to cry hard. You put your arm around her.

"Elise, what's wrong?"

"I don't know. I feel sad all the time. I'm always depressed. I can't control my depression. I can't stop being sad. All I want to do is cry all the time."

You want to help Elise, but you don't know how. You could talk to your mom, but she'd just call Elise's mom, and she won't do anything. You could talk to your youth pastor, but she's not the best counselor and might make Elise feel worse. You don't have any idea how to help her.

"I just want to be happy," she says. "I'm tired of being sad. I'd do anything to be happy for one day."

With Elise, you're not sure what that means. Would she try using a chemical to cure her sadness? Would she get into an unhealthy relationship with a guy? You're just not sure. All you know is that Elise is desperate to be happy. She seems willing to try anything.

Live It Strong

- What would you do to find out what's wrong with Elise?
- What would you do to help Elise?
- What have you learned this week that you could offer as advice for Elise?

171

God's Word

Now make confession to the LORD, the God of your fathers, and do his will. *Ezra 10:11*

Do nothing out of selfish ambition or vain conceit, but in humility consider others better than yourselves. *Philippians 2:3*

Avoid every kind of evil. *1 Thessalonians 5:22*

Live It

Managing your emotions can feel as hard as controlling a pile of snakes. You never know how you're going to feel. You're not sure how to deal with the emotions. You're confused about what to do about the way you feel. The thing about emotions is that people don't usually tell you how to deal with them. You'll probably never be given a book that tells you exactly how to handle the emotions you feel or experience.

Managing your emotions the right way isn't easy. How do you learn how to correctly handle your emotions? What comes close to the experience you face trying to handle your emotions? Try this.

Get two buckets and a spaghetti strainer that will fit into one of the buckets. Fill the bucket that the strainer fits in with water. Take both buckets outside and set them about ten yards apart. Stand by the bucket filled with water and put the spaghetti strainer in it. Here's your challenge: You've got ten minutes to use the spaghetti strainer to transport as much water as you can into the empty bucket. You might want to have someone time you to make sure you don't go over ten minutes. When you're finished, answer these questions.

1. How much water did you transport? _____
2. Were you frustrated using the strainer to transport the water?
   _____

Why Are Emotions
So Frustrating?

Trying to manage difficult emotions can be a lot like transporting water with a spaghetti strainer. You have a lot of emotions to handle, and sometimes it feels like you're not equipped to deal with it.

Imagine this: Each hole in the spaghetti strainer represents a moment when you couldn't manage your emotions. Each drop of water that didn't get transported is an emotion that you're not sure how to deal with. Managing your emotions can feel impossible—like transporting water in a spaghetti strainer. But here's good news. When you want to scream at someone, when you're feeling attacked, when you're in a bad mood and want to attack someone, you can rely on God.

How do you rely on God to help you with your emotions? First, ask God to help you handle your emotions. Second, consider the other person involved. If you are about to attack, yell, or fight, think about how you'd feel experiencing what you're about to give to someone else. Finally, consider removing yourself from the situation before you do something you'll regret.

Live It Strong

- What have you learned about handling your emotions from this activity?
- Using what you've learned from this activity, how would you explain the importance of handling your emotions to a friend?
- How can you apply what you've learned about your emotions from this illustration and from Scripture to your life?

WHY IS FEAR SUCH A BIG DEAL?

God's Word

Fear of man will prove to be a snare, but whoever trusts in the Lord is kept safe. Proverbs 29:25

I, even I, am he who comforts you. Who are you that you fear mortal men, the sons of men, who are but grass, that you forget the Lord your Maker, who stretched out the heavens and laid the foundations of the earth, that you live in constant terror every day because of the wrath of the oppressor, who is bent on destruction? For where is the wrath of the oppressor? Isaiah 51:12–13

And so we know and rely on the love God has for us. God is love. Whoever lives in love lives in God, and God in him. In this way, love is made complete among us so that we will have confidence on the day of judgment, because in this world we are like him. There is no fear in love. But perfect love drives out fear, because fear has to do with punishment. The one who fears is not made perfect in love. 1 John 4:16–18

Live It

"Dad? Would you check just one more time?"

"Honey, I've checked three times already. There are no monsters under your bed. Go to sleep."

"Could you check the closet, too, please?"

"Alright, I'll check the closet."

Your dad walks slowly to the closet, almost as if he's scared to discover what's behind the door. His hand trembles as he reaches for the doorknob. He slowly turns the handle, and then WHAMO! Your dad falls backward onto the ground, and you scream and dive under the covers. After a few seconds of yelling for your lives, the two of you crumple onto the bed, laughing. You do this every night. Tonight was one of the best ones yet.

Ever scared of the monsters under your bed? How about the ones in the closet? Okay, you've conquered the whole monster thing. Anything else freak you out? Make you really afraid? Take a moment and list your fears below.

_____

_____

_____

Fear is weird, isn't it? The strangest thing can scare you and keep you from making a decision or taking action. Just like the thought of a monster kept you glued to your bed when you were a kid, just the hint of failure keeps you from making a decision or acting on something God has told you to do. Fear—it's the huge scary invisible monster hiding in our closets that often prevents us from doing the things that are important for our survival.

Even though we know that God has conquered fear and even though we know that God is powerful, sometimes fear seems more real than God. Sometimes what we're afraid of seems more powerful than God.

This week we'll be focusing on fear. You don't have to be afraid. God has conquered the monster in your closet, and he wants you to know that you can call on him when you're afraid.

Live It Strong

- What are you afraid of? Why are you afraid of it?
- Why do we often let fear rule us?
- What can you do this week to recognize and conquer your fears?

God's Word

Then the man and his wife heard the sound of the LORD God as he was walking in the garden in the cool of the day, and they hid from the LORD God among the trees of the garden. But the LORD God called to the man, "Where are you?" Genesis 3:8–9

Have mercy on me, O God, according to your unfailing love; according to your great compassion blot out my transgressions. Wash away all my iniquity and cleanse me from my sin. Psalm 51:1–2

Now we know that whatever the law says, it says to those who are under the law, so that every mouth may be silenced and the whole world held accountable to God. Therefore no one will be declared righteous in his sight by observing the law; rather, through the law we become conscious of sin. Romans 3:19–20

Live It

We all came from somewhere, right? Have you ever read the first few chapters of Genesis and paid attention to the actions of the first humans? The crescendo of God's creation was his forming of the first humans. Adam and Eve had everything. Food. A garden. And a very close relationship with God. They weren't just formed by God's hands, they had close contact with him. Wouldn't that be amazing?

You probably already know the story about how Adam and Eve completely wrecked their close, intimate relationship with God. They sinned. First Eve believed the snake's lies, then Adam. When they sinned, Adam and Eve lost more than their cool garden (they got kicked out) and God's regular provision. They lost their close relationship with God.

When they sinned, Adam and Eve's first response was to hide. This seems like a weird move, if you think about it. These two had never sinned before, and they hadn't heard about someone else hiding after they had sinned because no one else existed before them. So why the strange attempt to hide from God? I think it reveals something about human nature. When we're guilty and we know we're guilty, we don't want God to know. We want to run away from God. We try to hide. Fear kicks in.

Maybe because he's important to us, and we don't want him to know how bad we've messed up. Maybe it's because we know that he can and will judge us for our sin. Our sin and fear together ruin a lot of stuff for us. We lose out on a great relationship. We end up looking silly as we try to hide from God. We miss so much just because we sin and then can't face God.

I've noticed something about the connection between sin, guilt, and fear. When I've sinned, felt guilty, and not done anything about it, I quickly forget my sin and begin to live with the guilt. After I've lived with the guilt for a while, fear creeps in. Then I begin to resent God for making me feel guilty and afraid—God didn't make me feel that way, but when we're really guilty, don't we usually try to blame someone else? Once I've started blaming God for my fear, sinning gets easier. Before long, staying away from God (not having devotions, not praying, not obeying his Word) is easier than running to him and asking forgiveness.

Have you ever felt like your hands were tied behind your back? You try to do something great and spiritual, and you mess up. You try to pray, but it feels like your prayers are just bouncing off the ceiling. You feel like God is a million miles away and getting back to him is impossible.

That's the result of your sin with guilt and fear mixed in. That's why confessing your sins to God is so important. Not confessing them and trying to hide from God doesn't just wreck your relationship with him, it affects your whole life. It not only keeps you from living for God, it keeps you from accomplishing what he wants you to do.

Live It Strong

- When have you tried to hide from God?
- What sins have you tried to ignore or forget?
- Why does it seem easier to ignore our sins rather than just confess them to God?

God's Word

Find rest, O my soul, in God alone; my hope comes from him. He alone is my rock and my salvation; he is my fortress, I will not be shaken. My salvation and my honor depend on God; he is my mighty rock, my refuge. Psalm 62:5–7

But those who hope in the LORD will renew their strength. They will soar on wings like eagles; they will run and not grow weary, they will walk and not be faint. Isaiah 40:31

But blessed is the man who trusts in the LORD, whose confidence is in him. He will be like a tree planted by the water that sends out its roots by the stream. It does not fear when heat comes; its leaves are always green. It has no worries in a year of drought and never fails to bear fruit. Jeremiah 17:7–8

Live It

Remember the first time you rode your bike without training wheels?

My youngest daughter has been begging me to teach her how to ride her bike without training wheels. She's dying to ride like her big sister. When you're a kid, a few things that happen to you signify that you're growing up and that you're really as big as you think you are, like learning to walk, potty training, and starting school. Learning to ride without training wheels is also a huge moment for a kid. It's a huge moment for my daughter. It's important to her.

So I had this plan.

I was a little nervous about taking off her training wheels all at once. Instead I took the bars that hold the training wheels in place and bent them up a little. That way Jessica would still have the wheels to rely on, but they'd only catch her when she leaned too far to one side. When she started riding on training wheels she had three wheels in the back holding her up. Gradually Jessica's bike has begun to look really strange with one big wheel and two smaller ones which are now bent up so high that they almost look like wings instead of wheels. She's slowly learning to rely only on the center wheel.

After I had first bent the wheels up, Jessica and I stood there looking at her bike. We were both amazed. Well, *I* was amazed . . . with myself. Honestly, I couldn't believe how smart I was. Instead of having to run behind my daughter while she learned to ride without training wheels, all I had to do was keep an eye on her while she learned on her own. I was brilliant.

As I stood there marveling at my idea, I looked down at Jessica. She had a different perspective. She didn't think I was a genius at all. She had one of those freaked-out-kid looks on her face. She wasn't confident, and she didn't think I was a genius. She wasn't overjoyed that I'd be inside the house staying cool and relaxing while she was outside alone trying not to bust her behind over my cool invention.

You can probably imagine what happened—or what didn't happen. I thought my wheel-bending idea meant that Jessica wouldn't actually have to keep her balance because the moment she leaned too much to one side, the training wheel would catch her. My theory, however, was all wrong. The wheels didn't catch, and she fell over a lot. Slowly Jessica's balance got better, and she learned to ride on her own in spite of my crazy idea, but it took a while.

We think that God loves to watch us lean too far over and fall off our bikes. We think that he loves it when we're afraid of him. We read in the Bible that we're supposed to fear God, and we think that means that we're supposed to be afraid of him. But I don't think that God wants us to be afraid of him—just to respect him. And I know he doesn't want us to be afraid of his plans for us, no matter how strange his plans sound and how difficult his will seems to accomplish.

When we're afraid of God, we can't really love him or even serve him. Jessica has taught me that even when you're afraid (or it seems like your dad has lost his marbles), it's okay to believe what your father tells you and go for it. I'm learning that even when my heavenly Father does something that I think is strange, I need to believe his plan, trust him, and just go for it.

Live It Strong

- Why are we afraid of God's plans for us?
- What things has God asked you to do that made you afraid?
- What should we do when we think God is asking too much from us?

God's Word

I, even I, am he who comforts you. Who are you that you fear mortal men, the sons of men, who are but grass, that you forget the LORD your Maker, who stretched out the heavens and laid the foundations of the earth, that you live in constant terror every day because of the wrath of the oppressor, who is bent on destruction? For where is the wrath of the oppressor? Isaiah 51:12–13

For we do not have a high priest who is unable to sympathize with our weaknesses, but we have one who has been tempted in every way, just as we are—yet was without sin. Hebrews 4:15

For he himself is our peace, who has made the two one and has destroyed the barrier, the dividing wall of hostility. Ephesians 2:14

Live It

Ever been in a prison camp? Ever been tortured? Ever been left to starve until you talked? Had your feet burned to coerce you into confessing?

Right now you're thinking, "He's nuts! No, I've never been in a prison camp, and I've never been tortured."

I bet you have.

Have you ever studied what they do to political prisoners in other countries or to people who have been kidnapped to get information from them? I've read up on it, and it's not pretty. Many organizations who report on the conditions of prisoners in third world countries report what they uncover on the Internet. Do a quick search and you'll find out they use a variety of torture tactics, things like:

- making them sit in the same position for days, causing some of their internal organs to fail
- forcing them to stand on one leg for hours
- making them lie facing the ground without touching the floor with anything but their fingertips and the tips of their toes

- interrogating them for many days in a row without allowing them to get any sleep
- beating them with all kinds of things

It's one thing to be held in prison for breaking the law. But it's an entirely different thing to be held, beaten, and tortured in prison when you haven't done anything wrong. I doubt any of us could take that, and I bet that if any of us knew someone who was being tortured in prison, we'd do whatever we could to help them. I bet we'd take whatever action we could to end the pain and agony of someone held against their will.

So here's the question: What's holding you prisoner? What's holding your friends prisoner?

Yeah, I know. You're not being physically tortured. You're not being tied to a chair. You're not being beaten. Your friends aren't being physically messed up either.

But what about the kind of torture that you can't see? Spiritual torture. Emotional torture. Psychological torture. Those kinds of things can be just as damaging as physical torture. You might not be beaten every day, and your friends might not be either. But you might be experiencing another kind of torture.

You see, Satan loves to make you afraid, and the fear he creates in your mind can feel like torture. Like you're walking on nails. Each step you take is painful. Each day is so filled with uncertainty and fear that it's just easier to stay in your room.

What do you do when Satan has succeeded in making you afraid of everything you do? I think that the best thing to do is to remember who God is. If we can remember that our loving heavenly Father can't stand it when we're afraid, then we'll remember that he can't stand the people who make us afraid. God shields us from the destruction Satan tries to hit us with because God loves us and can't stand to watch us live in fear.

Live It Strong

- What fears are holding you prisoner?
- When you notice that a friend is completely full of fear, what should you do to help him or her?
- How can remembering who God is help you break free from your fear?

God's Word

God is our refuge and strength, an ever-present help in trouble. Therefore we will not fear, though the earth give way and the mountains fall into the heart of the sea, though its waters roar and foam and the mountains quake with their surging. Psalm 46:1–3

I have been crucified with Christ and I no longer live, but Christ lives in me. The life I live in the body, I live by faith in the Son of God, who loved me and gave himself for me. Galatians 2:20

Let us fix our eyes on Jesus, the author and perfecter of our faith, who for the joy set before him endured the cross, scorning its shame, and sat down at the right hand of the throne of God. Hebrews 12:2

Live It

I have several heroes. One of my hugest heroes doesn't actually exist. Well, he *does* exist, but only in movies. It's Indiana Jones.

I've always thought Indiana Jones was the ultimate explorer. If you've ever seen any of the Indiana Jones movies, you know that he's the ultimate intellectual and at the same time the ultimate explorer. His movies are always full of wild adventures. He's the kind of guy I wish I was: intelligent, rugged, and most of all fearless. Nothing scares this guy. He faces the toughest moments without showing any fear.

The last Indiana Jones movie, *Indiana Jones and the Last Crusade,* involved Indiana searching for his kidnapped father and looking for the Holy Grail—the cup thought to be the one used by Christ at the Last Supper. Throughout the movie Indy has all kinds of really cool adventures and awesome moments. At the end of the movie, he has to face a series of difficult tests. He's been reunited with his father and has found the location of the Holy Grail. All Indy has to do is make it through a series of four tests, and he'll possess the Grail.

The tests aren't easy. First Indy has to pass through the entrance of a large tunnel without getting his head chopped off by sharp, moving blades. Then he has to cross a path without falling through the floor and down hundreds of feet. Next he has to have faith that a path he can't see actually exists and leap onto it. Finally Indy has to choose the correct cup from many cups. If he chooses the wrong cup, he will die a really awful death.

Because Indiana Jones is the hero (and because it's a movie), he beats the odds, makes it through all of the tests, and finds the actual cup of Christ. Even though it's a Hollywood portrayal of a fictional character, the way Indy faces his tests in a remarkable way has taught me a lot. He doesn't let the pain he might experience keep him from doing what he has to do. He doesn't let the danger in a situation keep him from acting or from doing what is right. Indiana Jones is a great (fictional) guy because fear doesn't rule him. In the made-up stories about his nonexistent life, he's able and willing to face whatever danger he needs to face in order to get the job done.

I know he doesn't really exist, but wouldn't you love to have his fearlessness? Wouldn't it be totally cool to be able to face anything, knowing that even though you might be a little afraid, that's nothing compared to your ability to tackle what you're facing? That's not the way it is for me. God sets out a plan, and my fear keeps me from accomplishing his plan. I know that's silly, since God's plans are always awesome. Still, my fear of the unknown and my belief that God's plan is just too tough prevent me from stepping out.

Chickens never accomplish much of anything. Their fear keeps them locked up. Their fear keeps them from doing anything for God. Can you live like Indiana Jones and face your fears with faith and boldness?

Live It Strong

- Is it easier for you to be a chicken or to face your fears? Why?
- Is it possible to live completely fearlessly? How?
- Why is it important to live fearlessly?

God's Word

You will not fear the terror of night, nor the arrow that flies by day, nor the pestilence that stalks in the darkness, nor the plague that destroys at midday. Psalm 91:5–6

Peace I leave with you; my peace I give you. I do not give to you as the world gives. Do not let your hearts be troubled and do not be afraid. John 14:27

So we say with confidence, "The Lord is my helper; I will not be afraid. What can man do to me?" Hebrews 13:6

Live It

If your parents knew where you were right now, you'd be completely busted.

Your boyfriend Luke talked you into going to the haunted house. And even though your parents have ordered you not to go to these kinds of things, Luke was being too flirty and persistent to ignore. Because of your parents' rules, you've never seen the inside of a haunted house.

So far the whole thing doesn't look that scary. The paint on the walls makes the place look cheesy. The makeup on the zombies doesn't convince you. And the noises, the fake graves, and the dude popping out of a coffin every now and then aren't that impressive. You're sure your parents didn't mean this kind of haunted house. This isn't haunted, and it's not even scary.

When you get home that night, your parents are sitting in the living room, and they both look very upset. Your dad starts.

"How'd it go tonight?"

"It was okay. We just hung out." Your parents hardly ever sit together in the same room. Something is up. Your mom looks at you and continues for your dad.

"Tell me about the haunted house."

At this point you can choose to gamble and lie to your parents or to just be honest. You pick the low road.

Why Is Fear
Such a Big Deal?

"Haunted house? We didn't go to any haunted house." You're caught and you're starting to feel guilty. You're hoping that your parents can't tell. Your dad obviously knows you're lying. Almost like he's on a tag team of prosecutors (who can smell guilt), your dad takes up the hunt again.

"Shelly's parents saw you there and called us. We know you were there. Don't try to deny it, and do not lie to us."

You immediately begin to cry. You feel a burning mix of guilt and fear. This isn't the first time you've disobeyed your parents, and it isn't the first time they've caught you breaking one of their rules.

It's the tag team thing again, so now your mom starts in.

"You know our rules. We don't want you going to haunted houses. You know they represent demonic things. Your father and I feel that going to those places opens you up to demonic activity. We don't want you to be affected by demonic elements."

"But mom, I don't believe in that. That kind of stuff can't affect me, and I was with my friends. Their parents let them go, and they're not freaking out about demonic stuff or anything. I'm sixteen, and you need to let me live a little."

Your parents don't take your words very well. They ground you and tell you not to hang out with the friends who took you to the haunted house.

Live It Strong

- Why do you think your parents are so upset?
- What effect do haunted houses or other demonic things have on our lives?
- Should we be afraid of spiritual things? Why is it important to be careful about them?

187

God's Word

I, even I, am he who comforts you. Who are you that you fear mortal men, the sons of men, who are but grass? Isaiah 51:12

How much more, then, will the blood of Christ, who through the eternal Spirit offered himself unblemished to God, cleanse our consciences from acts that lead to death, so that we may serve the living God! Hebrews 9:14

Let us draw near to God with a sincere heart in full assurance of faith, having our hearts sprinkled to cleanse us from a guilty conscience and having our bodies washed with pure water. Hebrews 10:22

Live It

If you made a list of the things that people were afraid of, you'd end up with a long list. Bugs. Guns. Flying. People are scared of all kinds of things.

What are you afraid of? What happens when you're afraid? What does your fear keep you from accomplishing?

If you're a normal person, fear paralyzes you from something. Think about it: Fear of failure will keep you from stretching and trying to reach your dream. Fear of making God angry can keep you from being honest with him. Fear of people can prevent you from making friends or from telling someone about Jesus. Fear can keep you from experiencing everything that God has for you. It can keep you locked in your room, unable to do anything that God asks.

Fear paralyzes us. God doesn't want you to be immobile and live your life in fear. So, how do you give up your fears and begin to live fearlessly for God? Try this.

Get a mask. It doesn't matter what kind of mask you get, but try to get one that's used for Halloween. If you can't find a mask, make one that looks scary. The mask represents the things that scare you. Once you've found or created the mask, put it in front of you. Imagine that the mask represents all the things you're afraid of and everything that keeps you from living fearlessly for God. Get a piece of paper and write

Why Is Fear
Such a Big Deal?

a list of the things that you're afraid of. These can be things that you wrote on the list for Day One of this week or other things that you think up. Don't be afraid to write as many things as you think up, and don't think any fear is too small to include. When you've made your list, tape it to the inside of the mask and put the mask somewhere in your room where you'll see it a lot. You might want to put it on your wall or on your desk—anywhere where you will notice it every day and be reminded of the list inside the mask.

Once you've found a safe location for the mask, spend time every day asking God to help you give up the fears inside the mask. Ask God to give you the strength to face the fears, and then pay attention to the ways that God makes you fearless. Throughout the week you might notice feeling more confident about a few of the things on your list. If you do, mark those things off your list, and praise God for giving you confidence and making you more fearless.

Live It Strong

- What have you learned this week about facing your fears?
- Why is it important to confess our fears to God?
- How can you apply what you've learned about handling your fears from this illustration and from Scripture to your life?

WHY SHOULD I LIVE IT STRONG?

God's Word

But you will receive power when the Holy Spirit comes on you; and you will be my witnesses in Jerusalem, and in all Judea and Samaria, and to the ends of the earth. Acts 1:8

But he said to me, "My grace is sufficient for you, for my power is made perfect in weakness." Therefore I will boast all the more gladly about my weaknesses, so that Christ's power may rest on me. 2 Corinthians 12:9

For God did not give us a spirit of timidity, but a spirit of power, of love and of self-discipline. 2 Timothy 1:7

Live It

Strength comes in all kinds of forms, and people use their strength in all kinds of ways.

If you're rich, you can use that strength to help homeless people or to build yourself a mansion. If you can bench-press 500 pounds, you can use that strength to lift cars off trapped people or to punch someone's face off. If you're smart, you can use that strength to create cures for killer diseases or to create bombs that wipe out generations of people.

You can do anything with the strength that God has given you. So brainstorm for a minute. What kind of things can you do for God if you're committed to live strongly for him? How can you impact the world? Whose life could you change if you chose to live boldly and strongly for God? Write down a few ideas.

_____

_____

_____

What does it mean to live strongly for God?

- It means using the gifts God has given you to further his kingdom.

Why Should I Live It Strong?

- It means devoting yourself completely to God.
- It means living off God's Word and reading it daily for direction.

Without strength, nothing gets accomplished. But using the strength and abilities that God has given you, you can change your life. You can change the world. All it takes is the determination to live strongly for God.

This week you'll be challenged to live for God with everything you've got. No excuses. No lying to yourself and saying that you can't do it. No fair copping out and not trying. This is about you, God, and his call on you to live strongly for him for the sake of your friends and your world.

Live It Strong

- What does it mean to live strongly for God?
- What are the benefits of living strongly?
- What can you do this week to live stronger for God?

193

God's Word

We who are strong ought to bear with the failings of the weak and not to please ourselves. Each of us should please his neighbor for his good, to build him up. Romans 15:1–2

To keep me from becoming conceited because of these surpassingly great revelations, there was given me a thorn in my flesh, a messenger of Satan, to torment me. Three times I pleaded with the Lord to take it away from me. But he said to me, "My grace is sufficient for you, for my power is made perfect in weakness." Therefore I will boast all the more gladly about my weaknesses, so that Christ's power may rest on me. That is why, for Christ's sake, I delight in weaknesses, in insults, in hardships, in persecutions, in difficulties. For when I am weak, then I am strong. 2 Corinthians 12:7–10

Therefore, strengthen your feeble arms and weak knees. Hebrews 12:12

Live It

Weakness.

That's not a word you'd ever want associated with you, is it? You'd never want to overhear, "_____ (insert your name here) sure is weak, huh? What a weak freak." You'd never want to known as a freak, and you sure wouldn't want to be called weak. Weakness means all kinds of things, and all of them are negative. If you're weak, you're often thought of as useless and not a productive member of society.

But before I get into the actual definitions of weakness, why don't you try to think up your own definition. Answer a few of these questions about weakness.

194

How would you define weakness? _____

_____

_____

_____

Why Should I
Live It Strong?

What causes weakness in someone? _____

_____

_____

What are the results of being weak? _____

_____

_____

Name three areas of your life that you feel are weak. These could
be physical, spiritual, or other areas you feel weak in.

1. _____

2. _____

3. _____

Webster's dictionary gives a wide variety of definitions describing
being weak, and none of them are positive. Some of Webster's definitions include "lacking strength; unable to resist external force; mentally
or intellectually deficient; not able to withstand temptation; not able to
function properly; not having external authority." Think about those
words. Do any of those phrases describe you? Do any of them describe
your relationship with God? Do they describe your character?

Weakness is a tough thing to grapple with. On one hand, we're human
and we're going to be weak, at least in some areas. It's unavoidable. On
the other hand, weakness doesn't have any place in the life of a believer,
because God wants to make us strong. He can't stand us living in weakness, and he loves to build up areas of our lives where we're weak.

If you're weak in any area of your life, that's an area that you need
to give to God. We should be able to live strongly for God because the
areas that make us weak are areas where God wants to build us up. God
wants to make us strong believers for him. It's our responsibility to turn
over our weakness to God so that we can live strongly for him.

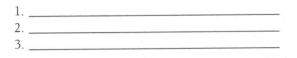

Live It Strong

- What areas of your life are your weakest?
- Why is it difficult to give our weaknesses to God?
- Why is it important to give God our weaknesses?

God's Word

The wicked man flees though no one pursues, but the righteous are as bold as a lion. Proverbs 28:1

His master replied, "Well done, good and faithful servant! You have been faithful with a few things; I will put you in charge of many things. Come and share your master's happiness!" Matthew 25:21

Now, Lord, consider their threats and enable your servants to speak your word with great boldness. Acts 4:29

Live It

I have a friend who is a full-time missionary. He's an extremely effective missionary, too. The people where he serves can be difficult to reach. He faces huge language barriers. The weather is often hot and uncomfortable. He serves in a part of the world where most Americans wouldn't want to live.

Halfway through his career as a missionary, Pete came to live in our city and attended our church. His passion and abilities were immediately evident. It's impossible to miss Pete. He's a large guy. He's got a huge voice. He's got a big personality. When Pete began attending our church, we knew that we had to get him involved. We invited Pete to talk to our youth group and college ministries and to preach on Sundays. We asked him to be involved in everything. And everywhere that Pete was involved, people began to change. When Pete talked to our college ministry, several in the group committed to being involved in full-time missions. When Pete preached in our pastor's absence, he preached from the perspective of a person in hell whose friends hadn't told him about Jesus. Many people in our congregation cried that morning as they remembered people they knew that weren't saved.

Pete's unashamed attitude and willingness to live strongly for God made an impact that changed our church. We haven't been the same since this guy went back to his mission field.

196

Since I hadn't followed his work before he went back, I figured that Pete would drift along on the mission field and not make much of a splash. I thought he might be bold in the U.S. but was probably not that bold or strong on the mission field.

I was totally wrong.

This man is amazingly strong in his walk with God, and he's an extremely effective missionary. I know, I've never seen him in action on the mission field, but the other day I got an e-mail from him that showed how strong he's living. He's been watching AIDS take over the lives of the people in the country that he serves. In his country thousands of people are dying of AIDS, and Pete's not the kind of guy who just stands around watching people die. So he's requesting that his special projects budget (an amount of money missionaries set aside for large projects that are unusually expensive) be used to start building an AIDS relief center.

This man who lived boldly, loudly, and strongly in the United States hasn't changed. He's living the exact same way in another country. It's safe to assume that Pete is affecting the lives of people just by being himself.

Your strong living makes an impact on others. You might not believe it, and you might not recognize it. But every time you step up for God—talk about him to others or do something powerful for him—you are impacting this world and you are impacting others.

Living strong for God. It won't mean fame or money. But it will mean that you'll make a difference in others.

Live It Strong

- Why is making a difference in others' lives important?
- What prevents you from impacting others?
- How does God feel when we make it a priority to impact others for him?

197

God's Word

For we are to God the aroma of Christ among those who are being saved and those who are perishing. To the one we are the smell of death; to the other, the fragrance of life. And who is equal to such a task? 2 Corinthians 2:15–16

Show proper respect to everyone: Love the brotherhood of believers, fear God, honor the king. 1 Peter 2:17

Dear friends, let us love one another, for love comes from God. Everyone who loves has been born of God and knows God. 1 John 4:7

Live It

Have you ever spent time with full-time missionaries? They're interesting and amazing people. I admire people who obey God and give up the opportunity to live in the United States to live in another country. Few countries outside the U.S. have all the comforts that we have. Missionaries possess an otherworldly ability to adjust to their adopted countries and live in uncomfortable conditions.

We have friends who went to work in Africa for a year. They didn't travel there to be missionaries. They actually went there to work in a university, helping with a particular program that the university wanted to start. While they lived there, our friends lived with the African people. They spent time getting to know them. They shopped at their markets, ate at their restaurants, played with their children. Our friends didn't go to Africa just to work and sightsee; they went to live among the African people.

When they got back to the U.S., we picked them up from the airport. It's about a three-hour drive from the airport to our house, and the whole way home we talked about their time in Africa. I asked about the missions opportunities there and what the missionaries were doing in Africa. Their response really threw me off. They told me that some missionaries were having huge success in explaining the gospel to African people. Other missionaries, they said, weren't making any difference at all. They said that some missionaries were having trouble adjusting to the cultural and lifestyle differences in Africa. Some missionaries couldn't stand the food. Others arrived in the country as "covert missionaries" (people who supposedly work in a company in Africa but are really missionaries), and their suspicious employment made many African people nervous.

The majority of the unsuccessful missionaries just couldn't stand being around African people. They hardly ever spent time with the people. When they did, they only did it to convert as many people as possible. Our friends told us that their experience in Africa was amazing. They said that the people are willing to listen to the gospel and are open to Christ. But they don't need people cramming the Bible down their throats. Instead, our friends found that if they were willing to hang out with African people, talk with them, and live boldly among them, then the African people were willing to talk about religion.

It's not really any different in the United States, is it? People don't want truth crammed down their throats. They don't want someone who can't stand their food or their country to give them advice about living or salvation.

How do you live strongly for God without turning off others and making yourself look silly? As you live strongly for God, remember that others are living their lives too. Sometimes it's best to simply love God and live for him in front of your friends and watch how they react to your life. Living for God doesn't mean being annoying, it means being devoted in a way that makes others infected by the way you live.

Live It Strong

- Why is loving others important?
- Why is it important to spend time with people we're trying to influence for Christ?
- How do we impact others without being annoying?

God's Word

There is a way that seems right to a man, but in the end it leads to death. Proverbs 16:25

I do not understand what I do. For what I want to do I do not do, but what I hate I do. And if I do what I do not want to do, I agree that the law is good. As it is, it is no longer I myself who do it, but it is sin living in me. Romans 7:15–17

Whoever claims to live in him must walk as Jesus did. 1 John 2:6

Live It

What would it be like to live life with boulders tied to ropes and hung around your neck? Imagine it. The weight. The embarrassment. Your back gets tired, but sitting down isn't an option since getting back up with boulders around your neck requires too much energy.

Nah, you don't wear rocks around your neck. No one does. It's true, only a super–strange, unintelligent person would tie boulders to ropes and walk around with that heavy necklace. But don't we wear things on our shoulders that prevent us from growing spiritually? Think about it:

- We carry sins that we don't want to give up.
- We carry worries about school that we don't know how to surrender.
- We carry anger at a friend or our parents that we feel justified to hang onto.
- We carry hurt about being ignored by a friend that we refuse to give up until they apologize to us.

No, you would never carry a rock on your shoulders for no reason. But I bet you carry other things that are just as heavy. Negative emotions. Sin. Disappointment. Worry. All those things weigh us down. And if we're weighed down, we can't live strongly for God. We have to learn to give up those things that weigh us down so we can live for God without the weight. How do we do that?

Turn things over to God. It sounds corny, but the more we say to God, "I can't handle this one—you take it," the more we grow and the lighter our load gets.

Run from temptation. How do we get such heavy loads? We never say no. We don't stop ourselves from sinning.

Listen to God. How do you know that the way you're living is wrong? How do you know that you need to change? God often speaks through his Word and through prayer times. Are you listening?

So many times Christians complain about their weaknesses but aren't willing to do anything about them. They walk around with no strength at all. They can't live strongly for God because they're too loaded down by their sin. Their ability to make an impact on others and to be bold is lost because they've believed that they're weak.

What about you? Do you know that others are watching you? They're learning how to live for Christ by watching you. They're learning how to stand strong for God by looking at your strength. They're learning how to live lives that aren't weighed down by sin by watching you and the way you live.

And more importantly, God is watching you. He's looking for the boulders you've got hanging around your neck, and he's grabbing at the rope to see if you'll let him pull the weight off. What do you live with that you shouldn't? What weight do you carry that you're not strong enough to bear? God wants to lift those off your shoulders, and he wants to see you living strongly and passionately for him.

Live It Strong

- What is the best way to turn things over to God? Prayer? Confessing them to your youth pastor?
- What weight are you carrying? Why are you hanging onto it?
- How will you let God have your weight?

201

God's Word

Do you not know that in a race all the runners run, but only one gets the prize? Run in such a way as to get the prize. 1 Corinthians 9:24

Not that I have already obtained all this, or have already been made perfect, but I press on to take hold of that for which Christ Jesus took hold of me. Brothers, I do not consider myself yet to have taken hold of it. But one thing I do: Forgetting what is behind and straining toward what is ahead, I press on toward the goal to win the prize for which God has called me heavenward in Christ Jesus. Philippians 3:12–14

I have fought the good fight, I have finished the race, I have kept the faith. 2 Timothy 4:7

Live It

Jeremy is notorious in your youth group. He's the guy who always parties on Friday and then shows up for youth group on Sunday night. Everyone knows about Jeremy's partying. Behind his back, people make fun of his double life. At school, Jeremy has a tough time. His church friends always seem to flock to him, because he really is fun to be around. But when his church friends hang around him, his partying friends get annoyed and make fun of Jeremy and his church friends.

One night last month Jeremy came to youth group and stopped you afterwards. The two of you got a burger and talked for hours about Jeremy's life. Jeremy is frustrated. Every time Friday comes around, his partying friends call and invite him to go out partying with them, and he usually can't resist. Then on Sunday afternoons he feels guilty, so he goes to church to feel better about what he's done.

You offer Jeremy some advice about how he can stand strong for God, but he doesn't seem willing to try. Jeremy wants to stop the cycle he's in but can't control himself. Instead of just giving him more advice, you decide to work out a strategy with him. You and Jeremy commit to pray about his unhealthy cycle of partying and churchgoing. You and Jeremy agree to meet together every morning before school starts to pray about his problem.

The following weekend you call Jeremy to see if he wants to rent a movie and hang out. You can't find him. He's not at home and his parents don't know where he is.

That Sunday Jeremy shows up at youth group. He looks fine, and he's hanging out, talking, and joking with everyone. When you say hi, he says hi back like nothing is wrong. You ask him how his weekend went, but he avoids the issue completely. After youth group, Jeremy asks if he can talk to you. So the two of you go out again to talk about his life. Jeremy tells you that he failed hugely in trying to not party. The two of you commit again to praying about Jeremy's problem, and Jeremy promises to try to keep his life straight.

Well, it's the weekend again, and once again you can't find Jeremy. You were invited to a party, and you figure Jeremy might be there. When you get to the house, you see Jeremy in the corner. He doesn't look like himself. He's acting weird and talking really loudly. You've never seen Jeremy drunk before, but you're sure that he's been drinking too much. Even though he's drunk and probably won't remember anything you say, you want to give Jeremy a piece of your mind.

Live It Strong

- What else could you do to help Jeremy with his temptations?
- How does giving in to temptation ruin our walk with God?
- Why is it important to not give up on friends who continually fail in their walk with God?

God's Word

*Commit to the LORD whatever you do, and your plans will succeed.
Proverbs 16:3*

*Since we have these promises, dear friends, let us purify ourselves from
everything that contaminates body and spirit, perfecting holiness out of
reverence for God. 2 Corinthians 7:1*

But just as he who called you is holy, so be holy in all you do. 1 Peter 1:15

Live It

One of the hardest things about living strongly for God is remembering your commitment. It's so easy to forget your commitment to God when you're faced with temptation or when that commitment seems inconvenient for you. When you forget him and give up on your commitment to God, you start living a weak life. When you live a weak life, everything goes into the tank. You start to sin a lot, you lose contact with God, you mess up in many ways.

How do you build a strong walk with God? How do you work on your weaknesses? I can't give you a simple solution. One size does not fit all. Not only is there no easy answer, but building your walk with God isn't easy. It's not like the solution comes in a bottle and all you have to do is drink it to instantly become a strong believer. It's an uphill walk. Where do you begin? Try this.

Get a rock. You've gotta get a big rock, one that you can use as a doorstop or that you'll notice somewhere else in your room. When you've got a big rock, paint the words *Live It Strong* on it. While you're letting the paint dry on the rock, get a sheet of paper and write down five areas of your life where you lack spiritual strength. These might be things that you've thought of throughout this week of devotions. When you've written your five things, tape the list to the bottom of the rock where no one will see it. As long as the rock with the list sits there in your room, use it to remind you to pray for your weak areas.

God doesn't want you walking around hanging your head like you're a failure or some kind of weak freak. He can't stand it when you make mistake after mistake. It breaks his heart to see you stuck in sin. When you commit your weaknesses to him and seek his healing for your weak areas, God doesn't just heal, rescue, and strengthen you. He sprints to your side and stays there because he wants to see you strong. He wants you to live as free from sin as possible. He wants you to stand with him—whole, healthy, and completely strong.

Live It Strong

- What have you learned about the importance of living strong for God from this activity?
- Using what you've learned from this activity, how would you explain how to live strong for God?
- How can you apply what you've learned about living strongly for God from this illustration and from Scripture to your life?

Tim Baker is a youth pastor and writer who has worked with teenagers for fifteen years. He is the author of six books, including the 2001 Gold Medallion winner *Extreme Faith* and the companion to this book, *Live It Loud*. He and his family live in Longview, Texas.